The Wildlife Sanctuary Garden

Also by Carol Buchanan:

Brother Crow, Sister Corn:
Traditional American Indian Gardening

The Wildlife Sanctuary Garden

Carol Buchanan

Ten Speed Press
Berkeley, California

A Kirsty Melville Book

Ten Speed Press
P.O. Box 7123
Berkeley, California 94707
www.tenspeed.com

Distributed in Australia by Simon and Schuster Australia, in Canada by Ten Speed Press Canada, in New Zealand by Southern Publishers Group, in South Africa by Real Books, in Southeast Asia by Berkeley Books, and in the United Kingdom and Europe by Airlift Books.

Illustrations by Bonnie Pollard
Interior design by Tasha Hall
Cover design by Nancy Austin

Art credits: Photos on pages 13, 14, 45, 49, 82, 111, 114, 138, 139, 140, 141, 142, and plates 1, 3, 4, 5, 6, 7, 10, 12, and 13 by R. Buchanan. Plate 2 by R. Buchanan, courtesy of the Rancho Santa Ana Botanical Garden. Photos on pages 71, 79, and plates 8, 9, and 11 by Carol Siipola. Plate 14 by Suse Greenstone. Illustrations on pages 6, 55, 61, 108, 121, 122, 125, and 130 by B. Pollard. Illustrations on pages 19, 28, 29, and 30 by B. Pollard, design by C. Buchanan.

Library of Congress Cataloging-in-Publication Data
    Buchanan, Carol, 1952–
       The wildlife sanctuary garden / Carol Buchanan
        p. cm.
    ISBN 1-58008-002-2 (alk. paper)
      1. Gardening to attract wildlife.   2. Sanctuary gardens.
    I. Title.
    QL59.B835 1999
    635.9'6—dc21   98-49793
                                     CIP

First printing, 1999
Printed in Canada

1 2 3 4 5 6 7 8 9 10 — 03 02 01 00 99

THE WILDLIFE SANCTUARY GARDEN is lovingly dedicated to Marilyn and Duane, who helped me learn early the meaning of stewardship.

Contents

Preface

I live with my husband, Dick, in west-
ern Washington, in the Puget Sound area, about twenty-five miles northeast of Seattle, where the hills start to rise out of the sound and Lake
Washington toward the Cascade Mountains. We average about thirty-
five inches of rain per year. Our climate is damp and drizzly for ten
months of the year, but for about two months—usually from late July to
late September—we get very little rain or no rain at all, and temperatures
may soar into the 90s and (rarely) top 100 degrees. Our home and,
consequently, our garden lie in an area called the "convergent zone," in
which warmer air from the south meets colder air from the north. As
a result, when it rains half an inch ten miles south of us, we may meas-
ure an inch to an inch-and-a-half in the same time period. It's a tricky
climate.

I've lived here nearly twenty years, but I grew up inland, in the
desert region of eastern Washington and in the mountain regions of
Idaho and Montana. As an adult, I've lived in the Midwest, in Southern
California, and in New York City. Also Dick and I have traveled exten-
sively in the United Kingdom and have visited more than once many of
the great gardens of England and Scotland. As a result, I have a fairly
wide experience of gardening in different climates from having lived and
traveled throughout the United States and abroad.

Sometimes I think I should write a book about gardening mistakes—
I've certainly made enough to fill a book or two! To save you from making the same mistakes, you'll find that I've been quite frank about the
things I've done wrong in the garden. My mistakes have come from not
having enough information or from doing things on impulse. I'm not
opposed to impulse as a way of making a garden—and I still buy plants
impulsively, sometimes—but I've found that the more information I
have, the better my impulses turn out these days.

In describing the principles of wildlife sanctuary gardening and how you might apply them, I've depended on my own experience, the experience of other wildlife gardeners, both locally and in the Wildlife Garden Forum on the Internet, and on what I've learned from reading and taking horticulture classes after work and on weekends. From living and traveling in different parts of the country, I've made observations about gardens and gardening that I draw on in the writing. I'm only one person, though, and my experience of gardening is not infinite.

But from living with a wildlife sanctuary garden for more than a decade, and from paying attention to what it has had to teach me, I decided to write this book, and Ten Speed decided to publish it, because there are few if any books that tell in depth of the author's own experience with this sort of garden. Since we've lived here, the garden has taught us some things I'd like to pass on in this book.

Of course, the United States is a big country. Some of the states are bigger than many countries. The nation is far too big and too complex, in terms of climate and plant life, for any one book to address all the details of gardening with native plants for wildlife in all regions, not to mention the hundreds of microclimates and plant communities that may exist in each region.

Yet certain basic principles apply, even with regional and local differences and with the inevitable exceptions, no matter what climate a person lives in.

First, be aware of the importance of using native plants to attract native wildlife. Second, understand the concept of plant communities. Third, control pests in the safest possible way. These three tenets form the core of this book.

You will inevitably have questions related to your own region and climate, and because one book can't be all things to all gardeners, I've provided you with the means of finding out the answers for yourselves. There's a saying that when you catch a fish for someone, you feed that person for a meal, but when you teach people how to fish, you feed them for a lifetime.

That's the ultimate aim of this book: to teach you what you need to know to enjoy a lifetime of wildlife sanctuary gardening and be able to find the answers you need to sustain that enjoyment.

Acknowledgments

*No book can ever be written and pro-*duced by just one person. These wildlife gardeners offered comments and advice based on their experience of wildlife gardening. To everyone, I'd like to say, "Thank you." If I've left anyone out, I apologize.

Bev Jernberg, Maryland

Susan Waterman, Alaska

Joseph Madrano, Washington

Frank Grazynski, Chairman, Trumbull Land Trust

Flora Skelly, Wild Ones, Washington

Karen Miles, Illinois

Tresa Newton, Alabama

These people added materially to the visual quality of the book:

Suse Greenstone, Pennsylvania

Carol Siipola, Washington

Bonnie Pollard, Washington

Dick Buchanan, Washington, who not only took smashing pictures, but engineered the garden infrastructure and actively lent his moral support to the project.

Chelsea Vaughn, Ten Speed editor, who exhibited great care and patience in early readings and throughout the production of the book.

Lessons from the Garden

When Dick and I moved into our house seventeen years ago, we were surrounded by second-growth forest. It had been logged off in the 1950s, but we thought the second-growth forest was idyllic. It was composed of alder, bigleaf maple, Douglas fir, western red cedars, western hemlocks, vine maple, ferns, berries, and salal. Though we could still see the stumps of the great old-growth trees, their replacements were huge. We loved the long hikes through the forest, and the area was still wild enough that a neighbor reported sighting a bear.

Naively, we little thought we were harbingers of an urban tsunami that was to swamp this hill. During the third winter, most of the forest surrounding us was bulldozed for housing developments. Several hundred acres of wildlife habitat disappeared. Only the scraps were left: a greenbelt just wide enough for a hiking trail, ten acres of woodland with trails preserved by a local riding group, a wetland bisected by a street. That winter was only a part of the urban sprawl that continues to devastate wildlife habitats in the Puget Sound region.

I was horrified and grieved that we had been part of the destruction. We took steps to, in a small way, make some restitution to the wildlife we had helped displace. As I now realize, in our ignorance we did some

1

things right for the wildlife and some things wrong. We put up bird feeders and installed a water garden as a year-round water source, but we uprooted the salmonberries that are a natural food supply. When we made the garden, although I planted roses and perennials in a mistaken effort to put in an English-style perennial garden, we kept most of the native plants: all of the ferns, two old stumps with huckleberries, the cascara trees, the towering bigleaf maples. From our first sight of the lot, we had loved the bigleaf maples, so we placed the house oddly, to preserve them. We have the only one-car garage on the hill, because a spectacular tree would have had to be cut down to make room for a two-car garage.

We did not put in a lawn, but we cut down all the alders because someone told us they were a "weed tree." True, we planted more trees: among them, three Douglas firs that are now much taller than the house. I read and studied and attended classes on native plants and botany and soils through the University of Washington's Center for Urban Horticulture and the area's community colleges. And I gardened.

I listened to the garden. I let it teach me what I needed to know. At first, I tried to imitate the perennial gardens of England (minus the lawn, of course). I'd make careful drawings on paper, just as the books say to do, select what appeared to be the right plants, and take good care of them. Still the garden looked nothing like the pictures in the books. The native plants flourished, and the exotics, the nonnatives, suffered.

The roses got mildew, black spot, and rust. Slugs devoured the delphiniums, and mold grayed the lupines. I thought I was a failure as a gardener. Eventually, I realized that the plants that were already adapted to this climate and the soil conditions in the garden were the happiest and took the least care.

That's what the garden had been telling me: The happy garden is in harmony with its climate and soil conditions. What I had been trying to do wasn't so far from the extreme example of the Southern California gardener who wanted to know how many ice cubes to put on the ground to give peonies the right amount of chill in winter. Going against nature just doesn't work. As a gardening friend said recently, "You can't fight city hall."

I gave up torturing plants, roses especially. When they suffered in this microclimate from too much shade and dampness, I took pity on them, dug them up, and gave them to friends who live in sunnier, drier parts of the Puget Sound region. In the roses' place I planted more native plants and compatible exotics such as dogwood shrubs, hardy cyclamen, hellebores, azaleas, and rhododendrons.

The more I stopped battling the elements to grow what did not belong here, the more the animals came. The garden changed from a poor imitation of a perennial garden to a wildlife garden supported by native plants. Some years later, in 1993, my garden received its official Washington State designation as a backyard wildlife sanctuary. The next year, because I had talked about it in the Compuserve Garden Forum, *Compuserve Magazine* became interested and featured it in the January 1994 issue.

Since then, our garden has become progressively more of a wildlife haven. Creatures that are safe nowhere else are safer here. Little by little, I've removed my interfering hands from parts of it. I watch more and listen. I try to hear what it's telling me. When a plant crops up, I watch to see what it does before I yank it out because I didn't put it there. In that way, I've gotten acquainted with some delightful natives: Watson's willow herb, with its beautiful little pink blossoms and gossamer seeds, and a native geum with five-petaled yellow flowers and two types of leaves. The basal leaves are rounded, the leaves on the stalks pointed.

The garden is teaching me to simplify. In the early stages, someone offended me greatly by calling the garden "fussy," but she was right. These days I fuss less, and the garden is less fussy, too. There are many fewer types of plants and more of the same sort of plant that seems to fit into the garden ecosystem. I confine my urge to fuss and putter to a large planter box and a couple of flower beds in the front. The garden is capable of living its own life, without my interference. I only intervene when it needs it—when shrubs need pruning, when weeds emerge in the pathways, when I decide that an unfamiliar plant really is a weed after all, when plants need water during our annual drought.

Over the years, I've learned two basic lessons from the garden:

First, a wildlife sanctuary garden really is a simple thing, made up of simple elements: food, water, shelter.

And second, a wildlife sanctuary garden is for both wildlife and people, a haven for you and your nondomesticated neighbors.

It took me years to realize that this whole proposition is really quite simple. So, as I said in the preface, I decided to write this book to encourage other people to do the same, to share with you what the garden has taught me, and to help you find the same joy we have found in this sort of gardening.

Throughout, I've used common and Latin names of plants. The common names are easier, but a plant can be known in different parts of this big country of ours by more than one common name. It will have only one Latin name. The Latin names can help you find the right plant at your local nursery.

Chapter 1 gives the principles the garden taught me, that underlie all the rest of the discussion in this book. Chapter 2 shows you how to design your own wildlife sanctuary garden, or how to help a professional design one that truly suits you and your situation. Chapter 3 discusses gardening with native plants. Chapter 4 tells how to attract critters to your garden. Chapter 5 shows you how to build a water garden. Chapter 6 offers some principles and guidance for keeping pests at bay. Chapter 7 describes the benefits others have received from this sort of gardening and the rewards that await you, too.

Because I don't have all the answers yet don't want to leave you at sea, chapter 8 will help you find the answers to your questions yourself. I've included an extensive list of information sources there. These sources draw more heavily on the Internet than on the public library, because I've been lucky at finding the latest continually evolving information at various Web sites. For example, the extension office for King and Pierce counties maintains a Web site called "Stewardship Gardening." I've provided the URL for each Web site. (*URL* is an acronym for *uniform resource locator,* the address of the file or Web site.)

I have only one caveat for the list of URLs. The Internet is crowded with information and Web pages, which are stored on computers called servers, because they serve as repositories of files that can be retrieved upon request from another computer. These servers are constantly being updated. As one becomes too loaded with information and runs out of room, another must be added and some files are moved onto it. This changes the address, or URL. When this book went to press the URLs were as accurate as they could be, but by the time you read it, some of the URLs may have changed. For this reason, chapter 8 also teaches you how to search the Internet for information in this area.

I hope you will find this book helpful as you go about making your own wildlife sanctuary garden.

Even Angus finds peace watching the birds—until a cat comes around.

Chapter 1

What Is a Wildlife Sanctuary Garden?

A wildlife sanctuary garden, no matter how small, is a haven for the wild creatures and the people who share the space. Without you and your family, it's not a garden; without the wildlife, it won't be a wildlife sanctuary.

A sanctuary garden will reward you hugely. In all seasons, it will have an extra dimension not found in most gardens. On warm summer days, in drizzly autumn, or in snowy winter, it will be alive with animals. The sight of them flitting and scurrying about, happily feasting or bathing or even squabbling, will brighten even the dullest mood.

A wildlife garden is a compromise between the purely natural, and the manmade. It is hospitable to wildlife, yet it is also for the people who live there, for you, your children, and your pets. Some people hold that the wildlife haven should be only for animals, as if human beings did not count in the scheme of things. That idea, it seems to me, looks at North America as if it had never been populated by people at all. Obviously, people were living here before European immigration, and they had their effect on the landscape, too. Indigenous people gardened, grew vegetables, tobacco, and orchards of fruit, and at times set forest fires to encourage berry plants to take hold in the aftermath.

People have long lived on this continent, but the original Americans had different ways of coping with nature than more recent arrivals have had. Immigrants brought with them the ideas of gardening formed in their home countries and cultures.

The Cultural Basis of American Yards

Prior to the early eighteenth century, Europeans, particularly of the English-speaking persuasion, assumed that the external, nonhuman world harbored evil and danger. Besides the physical dangers were the spiritual ones. People had believed for generations that the external world was a place of darkness and confusion, where devils lurked to ensnare the unwary. Folk beliefs spoke of trolls under bridges, and if educated people laughed at such stories, they nonetheless closed their doors and windows against the night air.

In the English language, the concept of nature as we understand it, meaning the nonhuman, material world, did not exist. According to the *Oxford English Dictionary, nature* first meant "the essential qualities and properties of a thing," and later, human nature. Not until 1662 did the word first appear in writing with what the OED has labeled its thirteenth meaning: "the material world, or its collective objects and phenomena, especially those with which man is more frequently in contact, the features and products of the earth itself, as contrasted with those of civilization."

The eighteenth century began in England with a collective national sigh of relief. The turmoil of the seventeenth century was over and royalty was once more firmly on the throne. Two revolutions, one violent and one peaceful, had replaced the Catholic Stuart line with the Protestant King William and Queen Mary in 1688. When Queen Anne succeeded to the throne in 1702, the educated classes settled down to enjoy the pursuits of peace, such as painting, poetry, and gardening. As they had revolted against the autocratic Stuart kings who had ruled during the sixteenth and seventeenth centuries, so now they revolted against what they perceived to be stilted formalism in the arts.

A group of wealthy young men who traveled to Rome and to Greece after the turmoil of the seventeenth century fell in love with the classical world. They sought artistic models in the arts of classical Rome, when a similar period of social stability during the reign of Caesar Augustus had led to an artistic golden age. Seeking to re-create that golden age, these young Englishmen imitated the classics in literature, painting, and gardening. They called themselves the "new classicists," or "neoclassicists." For them, nature meant something far different from the material world. Nature was defined by the neoclassicists as "the central idea and form which the particular struggles to attain." Or in less exalted terms, the world we perceive through our five senses is not reality, but an image of it. The rose a gardener grows is not the real one, but an imitation of the perfect flower that the gardener's rose is struggling to become, the ideal. It was a concept derived from classical literature, from Plato by way of Aristotle, from Homer, Virgil, and Pliny.

These young men came home from their journeys and, looking for the ideal hidden in the external forms, began to transform their estates into the ideal landscapes. They believed that ideal nature was primarily a mathematical concept and that nature was a matter of rectangles and circles. Their estates expressed this idea in the Palladian architecture. (In the United States we can see an example of Palladian architecture in Thomas Jefferson's home, Monticello.) The object of landscape gardening was to make the external world conform to the ideal. Nature was to be subdued, tamed, civilized. The wild was the enemy of civilization.

The Typical American Yard

To some extent, American culture, as seen in our yards, appears to hold that opinion still. The concept of taming nature, of reducing the external world to its mathematical essence, seems to live in the typical American yard. Our homes often have rectangular lawns that must be obeyed—mowed, fertilized, weeded, and mowed some more—before you can have fun. People rush to mow the lawn on weekends, before they can relax or play with their kids. When the children are older, parents and children fight over the lawn, in one of those unending battles that pass from generation to generation: "Mow the lawn or you can't go to the movies!"

Lawns cause a lot of worry, too. Where I live, in western Washington, people complain about moss in the lawn, and with an average of fifty-three sunny days per year, there will be moss. You can bank on it. Where you live there's probably something else—bindweed or crabgrass or mole hills—that someone's always combatting in the never-ending (but unspoken) contest to have the most perfect lawn on the street. In the arid West the green lawn consumes so much of a scarce resource— water—that its use for lawns is being seriously questioned.

Liberation!

As a beginning gardener, I battled nature, too. When we moved to our home in Washington, my only idea of gardening was the American model: a lawn and a vegetable garden, with a few shrubs around the foundation of the house. Then Dick, my husband, and I made our first trip to England, and I came back with an inner eye full of the beauty of English perennial gardens. As I sought to make something of the sort here, I found myself in a constant war against this tricky climate. People said the garden was beautiful, but I wasn't having much fun. I was its slave, and I spent too much money on it, another source of stress.

Eventually, I relaxed and decided to go with nature, rather than fighting it. When I came to that realization, I felt liberated. I began to turn the garden back, if not to its original state, at least to a garden much different than I had set out to make. Fortunately, we had never put in a lawn, so we had relatively little to undo. When we first moved in, we had laid out the basic shape of the garden, and kept most of the native trees and some of the shrubs. The revision has been more a matter of putting plants compatible with the climate into the existing structure.

In deciding not to imitate English perennial gardens, we haven't done away with garden color. Something is in bloom every month of the year, but for much of the year the garden is primarily green, one of the most peaceful colors. Both animals and plants flourish and reward us in their own ways, with happy antics and consistent bloom. Our guests often comment on how peaceful the garden is now. Children love it because it's interesting and it's like being in the woods. They play tag along the paths and throw the dog's ball in the larger patio.

Over the course of the last dozen years, we have helped our garden become a wildlife garden, in essence giving it back to the animals and plants, while still living there. We now consider ourselves stewards of the property for those without the words to speak for themselves. Another name for this type of gardening might be stewardship gardening.

A National Grassroots Effort

We aren't alone in this effort, either. The nation seems to be finding itself in the midst of a revolution in garden thinking, in a kind of grassroots (pardon the phrase!) movement made up of gardeners all over the country. Partly as a reaction against the urban sprawl and agribusiness that have taken the biggest toll on the natural world, farmers are learning methods of sustainable agriculture that will help preserve the planet for future generations, and we urban dwellers are beginning to recognize the need to do the same. Rather than recreating the indoors outside, we seem to be more willing to let the outdoors be the outdoors, which also makes a great deal less work.

Relax

With a wildlife sanctuary garden you can relax. In fact, if there's a watchword for this type of garden it's that: Relax. You can kick back if you want to. There are always weeds to pull, but you don't necessarily have to pull them. If a weed flowers, somebody will feast on the nectar. If not, one critter or another will feed on the leaves or shelter under it or around it, or a bird will eat the seeds. How tidy you want your sanctuary to be is up to you.

Our garden isn't fussy anymore. Sometimes a weed is a weed; sometimes it's a native plant. It depends on where it is, what it is, and what sort of mood I'm in. Dick and I have a deal: Anything growing in the gravel paths or patios is a weed. That way he knows what to pull and what not to pull. We all strike a balance that suits our situation. You will, too.

Sometimes I'm moved to tidy up, but I generally resist it. I try to confine my activities to those that will help the garden. I rake leaves from places they might smother plants and from the paths and patios. I prune shrubs and smaller trees for their health first and secondarily for their appearance. Mostly, I just sit in the garden and read or write. I enjoy my garden; it regenerates nerves jangled from the stresses of corporate life.

Besides, being too tidy isn't a very good idea for the animals. They may hide in leaves or overgrown plants. A case in point: Our garden has lots of native sword ferns. Last year's fronds dry out, turn brown, and sag to the ground in the summer. Eventually, they become part of the soil in which the fern grows. (In nature, plants grow in their own litter.) Some people clip off these older fronds, thinking that they are unsightly and the plants look better without them. I don't do that, very often, and when I do, it's usually in the front yard, where a really untidy look might offend the neighbors.

Recently, I accidentally moved a bit too close to a fern for the comfort of the very young possum that had hidden under the sagging fronds. A couple of days before, I had buried two other small possums just its size. Apparently, something had happened to the mother, and three of her babies found sanctuary in our garden. For two of them, it was too late. This one, however, might survive.

I hoped I wouldn't be burying this possum, too. I moved away from the plant so as not to disturb the possum. I saw it two more times, once early in the morning as it walked along the branch of a tree and one afternoon as it sipped water from one of our ponds. By the end of the summer it had doubled its size, so maybe it has a good chance. It doesn't have to forage far for food and water, so the danger to it is minimized. With the dense canopy of leaves overhead, a hawk will have a hard time finding the possum. It has food and water and shelter, so it has a good chance of surviving. I hope.

After all, this wildlife sanctuary garden is an Eden of sorts. It's peaceful. Birds sing, and the little waterfall gurgles. Birds chirp and twitter and splash in the ponds. Over the fence come the outside sounds of children laughing, dogs barking, people calling to each other. The lawn mowers roar, but not for long, and mostly on late Saturday afternoons. Pretty soon, all is quiet again. I read, sip, nibble. Every so often I look up to enjoy the play of light in the green leaves, in the red or yellow flowers. I hear the sounds of squirrel paws or the flutter of bird wings in the water. On hot days the garden is ten to fifteen degrees cooler than surrounding yards. (I've measured that difference.)

This young orphaned possum found sanctuary in our garden.

It's a friendly garden, too. Neighborhood children love to watch us feed the fish in the ponds. When we have friends in, we hope for weather good enough to sit outside, even if we have to wear jackets, even if for only a little while. We sit in the larger of the two patios. We put our feet up and talk and munch and sip. Time passes. The heat of the day disappears. When a squirrel or bird comes in, we stop talking to watch it. Frogs serenade us. At night the raccoons and possums come out to forage. That's about as wild as our wildlife is.

Size Is Irrelevant

Ours is not a big garden. It's just a good-sized suburban lot, shaped like a frying pan, with the pan part about 90 feet by 100 feet. In all, it's roughly 12,000 square feet. However, size is meaningless. The Washington State Department of Fish and Wildlife, for example, has certified every size property, from rural acreages to city balconies. Our friends Roxie and Denis have made a six-by-twelve-foot patch behind their condominium into a bird sanctuary by hanging feeders in the screening trees and filling a birdbath (see photo below).

If you live in an apartment, your lanai or balcony can also be a refuge for you and the creatures around you. All it takes are a pot or two of plants to attract pollinators, one or two bird feeders, a birdbath, and a birdhouse or some plants for shelter. Whether it's a balcony in Queens, New York, a suburban lot in Claremont, California, or acreage in the Flathead Valley of Montana, you can have a wildlife sanctuary garden.

Basic Principles

No matter what size you're working with, certain principles apply. The food sources should be those that animals recognize, so the plantings suggested in this book will be mostly native plants. Pollinators such as hummingbirds, butterflies, and bees, however, aren't fussy about native or nonnative plants. They'll happily draw nectar from any plant they

Even a small space like this can be a charming haven for both you and wildlife.

recognize as food. We have both native and nonnative honeysuckles, and the hummers eat from both.

Plants depend on each other for sustenance and protection. They compete with each other, too, for nutrients, moisture, and light. This relationship of dependency and competition makes a plant community, and the plant community, together with its animals, forms an ecosystem.

While the focus of this book is on getting as close to an ecosystem as you can, it doesn't take a purist's approach. Anything you do for your haven is better than nothing. A couple of feeders and a birdbath are better than no feeders and no water. A windowbox of flowers for butterflies and bees is better than no flowers for them and other pollinators.

A Dissonant Note

Somewhere along the way, you'll discover that nature isn't always cute. A hawk may swoop in and grab that cute squirrel or pretty bird you've been watching. You may bury dead baby animals, as I buried the baby possums, or see some animal suffering. If you can, try to restrain your kindhearted efforts to interfere with nature. Rescuing the weakest of a litter and hand-feeding it does nothing for the long-term survival of the species.

I haven't put the little possum in a box for hand-feeding. That would terrify it. In providing a haven for its survival, I'm letting the wild creature remain wild. If it survives, it won't be so dependent on humans that it will be unable to survive in the wild without us. It will still maintain that innate caution that warns it that some of us may be dangerous. If I were to hand-feed it, I would only delay its inevitable death by starvation or from some hardhearted person.

Be prepared at times to have your heart wrung, but remember, too, that building a sanctuary garden is the right thing to do, given the dire state of wildlife habitats on the planet as a whole. The loss of habitat means the loss of many types of plants and animals, and perhaps threatens our existence as well. We may feel powerless on a global scale, but we can affect what goes on inside our own boundaries. And one yard multiplied by thousands is a lot of habitat for creatures endangered by the loss of theirs.

What You Can Do Now

While you're learning about your space and investigating the sources of information provided in chapter 8, you can do some things immediately to minimize the problems for wild creatures and for your family, like ending lawn treatments. Pesticides and commercial fertilizers on lawns seep down into the ground and are carried in the groundwater to the water table or into the water system. Eventually, these chemicals work their way back into your drinking water. Even in trace amounts they may build up over time and affect your family's health.

Exchange your gas mower for a push mower and get the benefits of the aerobics. Put up one or two feeders and keep a birdbath filled and clean at all times. Don't pull out existing plants that some animal might have come to rely on for nectar or seed. Gradually, you can decrease the size of your lawn and plant colorful flowers to attract pollinators.

Keep in mind that some creatures may already have made their homes on your property. Slower changes to your existing garden are better for them, and proceeding slowly enables you to enjoy each phase. Read about what birds, bees, frogs, and butterflies like. Make mistakes and learn from them. Let things happen. Throughout the life of our garden, learning has been a continuous source of fun.

Why Make a Wildlife Sanctuary Garden?

Ultimately, fun is the best reason for building a wildlife sanctuary garden. We began by trying to make an English perennial garden, then turned it into a sanctuary garden partly out of guilt and partly to stop the sheer labor of battling the climate. Now we would start out this way because it's such great fun. Do it for the sheer joy of it. Do it for your pleasure. I promise you, it's the most rewarding garden you'll ever have.

Chapter 2

Designing a Sanctuary Garden

A few years ago, at a lecture, Penelope Hobhouse, the eminent designer of English gardens, said, "Gardens are a work of art and nature has nothing to do with it!" How times have changed. In the May 1998 issue of *The Garden,* the journal of the Royal Horticultural Society, John Brookes, the chairman of the Society of Garden Designers foresees "a newer, more flowing type of garden. . . . The plants chosen will relate much more closely to the garden's location, reflecting the local flora." He continues, "The overall feel will be more organic and free—with natural-looking areas of water for wildlife—and lots of winter interest with hips and berries for birds."

He is describing the basics of designing a wildlife garden.

Before you can feel comfortable with the idea of a wildlife garden, you must understand and be comfortable with two concepts: the wildlife garden aesthetic and plant communities. Before we get into the actual steps to designing a wildlife garden, I'd like to explore these concepts, so you can understand where the designs might take your garden. First, the wildlife garden aesthetic is a different look than Americans are used to. Second, plant communities are the basis of the design, in my view, so understanding them will be very helpful to you as you design your own garden. Reading these sections before you read about the design process will give you some background and understanding of where I'm coming from. Of course, feel free to jump ahead and read up on the design process first, then come back to these sections.

The Wildlife Garden Aesthetic

"Work where you can in the spirit of nature, with the invisible hand of art." The English poet William Wordsworth (1770–1850) recommended this approach in a letter to a friend in 1805. When he wrote that, he was a voice crying in the wind. He was revolting against the "improvers," who were themselves revolting against the neoclassicists described in the first chapter. The improvers were led first by Lancelot "Capability" Brown, who sought to improve on nature with smooth lawns dotted with clumps of trees and gently undulating streams. Wordsworth, attuned to the beauty of the natural landscape, hated these "improvements," but it's always difficult to go against prevailing fashion. Later on in the nineteenth century, his ideas had more influence, but it has taken until now for people to understand that what he meant by the spirit of nature was the wildlife garden.

The beauty of a wildlife garden is that of nature, with the "invisible hand of art." That invisible hand is in the design, the structure of the garden, and the placement of plants to reflect natural groupings, or plant communities. Our garden is in western Washington, naturally a heavily forested part of the state. Fortunately for us, when our immediate area was developed, the developers preserved a greenbelt with a walking trail through the length of it. The greenbelt runs less than a block from our house and loops around in a ten-acre forested area at the top of the hill nearly three miles away. When I want to know how nature would handle a garden question, like Wordsworth I have only to walk out and see. From the greenbelt I have learned what are the plant communities of the immediate vicinity.

One of Dick's best contributions to the garden, probably because of his engineering background, has been its strong structure. Clearly defined pathways and open spaces curve around the house. In Wordsworth's own gardens also, structure is much in evidence. He built terraces, long level pathways founded on rock walls in the steep hillsides,

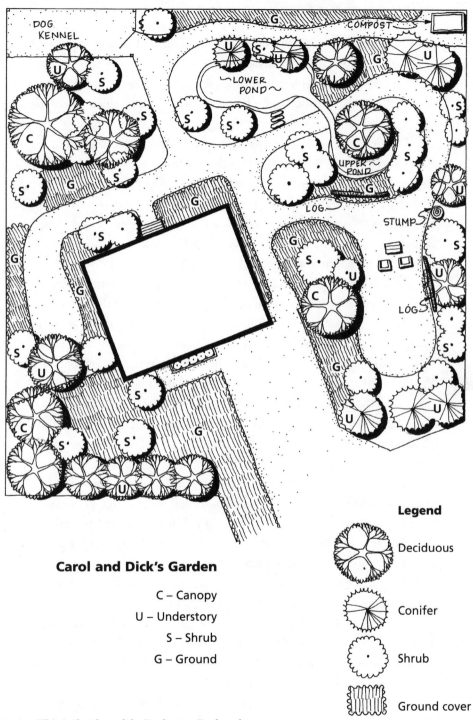

DOG KENNEL

G

COMPOST

LOWER POND

UPPER POND

LOG

STUMP

LOG

Carol and Dick's Garden

C – Canopy
U – Understory
S – Shrub
G – Ground

This is the plan of the Buchanan Backyard Wildlife Sanctuary.

Legend

Deciduous

Conifer

Shrub

Ground cover

on which people could walk through the gardens and enjoy the beauty of nature. On these terraces he composed his poetry, setting the rhythms with his feet and chanting them aloud. Lawn mowers hadn't been invented yet, so grass was cut by hand with a scythe or a sickle. By modern standards, his lawn was quite shaggy.

The beauty of wildlife gardens like Wordsworth's results not from drifts of color, as in the perennial garden, or from bold effects, but from its subtlety, from being in harmony with the surrounding landscape. That harmony arises from the use of native plants or compatible exotics. (A native plant may be thought of as one that was here—wherever "here" is for you—before immigrant settlers arrived in your area. An exotic is a plant that did not originate in the local area.)

Even in the concrete and glass canyons of New York City, Atlanta, or Los Angeles, the wildlife garden can reflect the landscape that once was. Northeastern wildflowers and shrubs might be used in New York, Southern plants in Atlanta, and desert plants in Los Angeles. In western Washington a wildlife garden is a matter of texture; with conifers contrasting with maple trees, and the gleam of dogwood bracts and madrona blossoms shining out of the cool, dim forest. In Southwestern deserts, a wildlife garden has bold lines and strong shapes, with subtle shades of blue-green and gray punctuated by yellow or red flowers. It is almost architectural.

A wildlife garden's beauty does not come from its tidiness. Ours couldn't differ more from the usual controlled, firmly edged lawns and narrow, disciplined flower beds like little Lincoln beards around the foundations of a house. Rather than making the outside look like the inside of a house, we've modeled the garden on nature itself. It usually looks slightly tousled. Leaves gather in corners, and I haven't raked behind some shrubs in years. Nor do I intend to.

The slightly scruffy appearance of the garden has a purpose. Fallen logs provide food for northern flickers, who hammer at the wood and break it down into pieces that decompose into the soil. Wild creatures and ground-nesting birds need untidy corners to shelter in. If I rake, I'll disturb a nest or food cache or hibernation spot. Fallen leaves decompose and become part of the soil, in a constant renewal that saves us from buying commercial fertilizers.

Weeds that aren't pulled immediately might become a prized plant. I leave them alone long enough to find out, anyway. Sometimes I regret that, but I've found some treasures that way, too.

Despite the haphazard look of a meadow or forest or wetland, natural places are anything but haphazard. They have evolved into a balanced, self-sustaining mutual interdependence between plants and animals. Trees seed, take root, grow, and die. Grubs munch on dead wood, and in turn woodpeckers eat the grubs for dinner (and probably breakfast and lunch, too). Shrubs and herbaceous plants bud out, and flowers form. Bees, butterflies, and hummingbirds go after the nectar, and as they move from flower to flower, they pollinate the plant and make possible the production of seeds for new plants. Eventually, the flowers fade and seeds form. Seed-eating birds dine on them. Mammals and hawks feast on smaller birds and smaller mammals and fish. And so it goes right on up to the top of the food chain, in a never-ending cycle of interdependence that brings life out of death for both plants and animals.

This is what we're aiming for in our garden. That's what wildlife havens are ultimately about—letting natural processes take place for the good of the wild creatures, all of whom know the score. This is the purpose of the wildlife garden aesthetic. Once you understand why it should look a bit unkempt, you can better appreciate it.

Plant Communities

Another element in the beauty of a wildlife garden comes from the use of plant communities, plant groupings that reflect or imitate what we would find in the nearby area. A plant community is a group of plants that grow together and have evolved naturally into an interdependent system.

Four Tiers

In a forest, the community is commonly in four tiers: canopy, understory, shrub, and ground. The canopy layer is composed of the tallest trees, those growing taller than fifty feet. Understory trees grow to between twenty and fifty feet tall. The maximum height of shrubs, twenty or twenty-five feet, overlaps with understory trees. Ground plants include ground covers and perennials that seldom reach more than three feet tall.

The concept is relative to the area. If you do not live in a forested area, or in what once was a forested area, you can still identify plant communities. In a wetland, the four tiers may still be present, but the tallest tier may be the height of the bulrushes at the edge of the water. In a meadow, the canopy layer might be the tallest grasses. In some desert areas, a saguaro cactus or juniper or piñon pine might form the canopy layer, with other plants growing around it.

Plant communities are constantly evolving, too, as species compete with each other for available resources of light, moisture, and nutrients. In the greenbelt, a stand of Douglas fir and western hemlock at the edge of a wetland is so dense that nothing grows on the forest floor in their heavy shade. Yet not many feet away, where more sunlight penetrates and the ground rises, ferns, salal, alder, and vine maple flourish.

A plant's age may also have something to do with its position in the canopy, understory, or shrub layer. At successive stages of its growth, a tree as towering as a Douglas fir may be part of the shrub and understory layers until it emerges from the shade of the current canopy trees. Then it becomes part of the canopy.

You can expect similar changes in your garden. Over time, larger trees may shade out smaller ones. A red flowering cherry that we planted during the second year of the garden has grown almost entirely in one direction as the native cascara and bigleaf maple trees around it have blocked the sunlight on the other sides.

Plant communities differ from one area to another, not only in the regions of the country, but within regions from one microclimate to another. Only in parts of the Puget Sound region, for example, do native madrona trees grow as understory trees beneath Douglas fir. In other parts of the area, these trees are not found naturally. They appear to need warmer temperatures and less moisture in the air. Where native plants are not found naturally, you might have more trouble growing them. On the other hand, two species of Oregon grape—one native to this area and the other to Oregon—do equally well in gardens here and in Britain, where they were introduced to English gardens in the early 1820s. (The local species is *Mahonia nervosa;* the Oregon native is *Mahonia aquifolium.*)

In our garden, plant communities imitate those found in the forest. In our immediate woods, the canopy trees are the great conifers: Douglas fir (*Pseudotsuga menziesii*), western red cedar (*Thuja plicata*) and western hemlock (*Tsuga heterophylla*), all of which can exceed 100 feet. Where the Douglas fir has not shaded them out, the deciduous bigleaf maples grow to about eighty feet. Understory trees include alders (*Alnus rubra*) and dogwoods (*Cornus sericea*) and cascara (*Rhamnus purshiana*). Our lot is blessed with two rare cascara trees that are now taller than the two-story house and may be near their maximum height of thirty feet. Vine maples (*Acer circinatum*) may be either tall shrubs or small trees. An array of edible berry plants—thimbleberry (*Rubus parviflorus*), salmonberry (*Rubus spectabilis*), and red huckleberry (*Vaccinium parvifolium*)—provide treats for animals in the shrub layer. Indian plum (*Oemleria cerasiformis*) blooms earliest in the forest. Salal (*Gaultheria shallon*), sword ferns (*Polystichum munitum*), dwarf bleeding hearts (*Dicentra formosa*), and shy trillium (*Trillium ovatum*) join other plants in the ground layer.

A wildlife garden reflects its natural surroundings in the use of plant communities. Our garden, which depends on a mixture of native plants and compatible exotics, is a woodsy garden because this area is wooded. On our plan shown on page 19, you can see how the four layers of the plant communities work together. The canopy trees are the native Douglas fir, western red cedar, and bigleaf maples. The understory trees include the native cascara trees and vine maples as well as some compatible exotics such as the thundercloud flowering plum put in because its red foliage adds color interest. The shrub layer is composed of native huckleberries, elderberries, thimbleberries, and some salmonberries. Along with these are rhododendrons, azaleas, and other exotic flowering shrubs. The ground layer is made up of salal, sword ferns, Japanese anemones, asters, and (in very shady areas) a spreading carpet of exotic hardy cyclamen.

When designing the plan for the canopy trees in your haven, keep in mind that living with big trees may present some special problems, so take the time to learn about them and be sure you want to take them on before you introduce them to your yard. Their size can be overwhelming; some trees spread to one-half to two-thirds of their height. Our big trees—bigleaf maple, Douglas fir, and western red cedar—commonly lose their lower limbs as they get big, so the spread is more noticeable higher up as they shade the ground below.

In England, however, I have seen some very old beech trees that would occupy fully half of our lot. Rather than have to cut down a beautiful tree when it matures, I'd recommend planting smaller ones to begin with. It's much less mess and expense in the long run. And also, I love big old trees.

What follow are some suggestions for how you might make the concept of plant communities work for your garden design.

The Northeast

For Northeastern gardens, including those in Appalachia, some canopy selections might include the various spruces; eastern white pine (*Pinus strobus*), at fifty to eighty feet; balsam fir (*Abies balsamea*), at forty-five to seventy-five feet; or larch or tamarack (*Larix larusina*), at forty to eighty feet. Where soils are moist, you might plant balsam fir or tamarack. Species of larch or tamarack are found throughout the mountainous regions of the Northern Tier, a band of northern states along the forty-eighth parallel from the Atlantic to the Pacific oceans. These trees are noted for their soft summer appearance, their brilliant yellow fall color, and their stark black winter skeletons. Tamarack is the only conifer that is not evergreen.

The heights of some of these trees indicate that they may be used in either the canopy or understory. However, if your space is limited, it's better not to plant any tree with the expectation that it stay within certain height limits. It might prove extremely happy in your garden and grow to its maximum height.

Among deciduous trees, two possibilities for the canopy layer might be the sugar maple (*Acer saccharum*) and the beech (*Fagus grandiflora*). The beech can grow to fifty to seventy feet, and in the wild to about 100 feet. Sugar maples may grow to sixty to seventy-five feet or more.

In either the canopy or understory layer, you might use the red maple (*Acer rubrum*) at forty to sixty feet and the paper birch (*Betula papyrifera*) at sixty to seventy feet. In the wild, they may be part of the understory with larger trees, but in the smaller garden one or two may serve as the canopy layer.

Many beautiful shrubs suggest themselves for the garden shrub layer. These include Labrador tea (*Ledum groenlandicum*), blueberry (*Vaccinium angustifolium*), and mountain holly (*Nemopanthus mucronatus*), which is not really a holly at all. Another possibility might be a rhododendron native to Canada: *Rhododendron canadense.*

For the ground layer you might try wood sorrel (*Oxalis montana*), starflower (*Trientalis borealis*), or bunchberry (*Cornus canadensis*), also known in some areas as creeping dogwood.

The Midwest

If you live in the Midwest, the canopy layer might include the eastern red cedar (*Juniperus virginiana*) or the northern pin oak (*Quercus macrocarpa*), both of which grow to fifty to seventy-five feet. The quaking aspen (*Populus tremuloides*), at thirty-five to fifty feet, could be used as either a large understory tree in a larger garden or a canopy tree in a smaller one.

Some examples of understory trees might include the American plum (*Prunus americana*), which grows to approximately thirty-five feet; the prairie or Iowa crab apple (*Malus ioensis*), at twenty-five feet; or the common chokecherry (*Prunus virginiana*), at thirty-five to fifty feet.

The Midwest has many beautiful native shrubs that provide interest as well as food for both humans and birds year-round. Among them are the Missouri gooseberry (*Ribes missouriense*) and the western snowberry (*Symphoricarpos occidentalis*).

The Southeast

Like other areas of the country, the South is made up of many different regions. For gardens in north Georgia, the eastern white pine (*Pinus strobus*), at 60 feet (120 feet in the wild); red maple (*Acer rubrum*), at 60 feet; and sweet bay (*Magnolia virginiana*), at 60 feet, might be possibilities for canopy plantings.

Some smaller trees in the South might include the southern red buckeye (*Aesculus pavia*), at fifteen feet; the Carolina cherry laurel (*Prunus caroliniana*), at twenty-five feet; Fraser magnolia (*Magnolia fraseri*), at forty feet; as well as the American holly (*Ilex opaca*).

For the shrub layer, you might consider *Cotoneaster dammeri,* or *Gardenia jasminoides,* the Cape jasmine. Or you might plant one of the several species of rhododendron and azalea native to the South and warmer parts of the eastern seaboard. These include *Rhododendron alabamense, R. arborescens, R. atlanticum, R. austrinum, R. bakeri, R. carolinianum, R. catawbiense, R. chapmanii* (native to western Florida), *R. flammeum, R. maximum, R. oblongifolium, R. periclymenoides, R. prunifolium, R. serrulatum, R. vaseyi* (native to eastern South Carolina), and *R. viscosum.*

The ground layer might include such woody vines as Carolina jessamine (*Gelsemium sempervirens*) or confederate jasmine (*Trachelospermum jasminoides*).

The Desert

For desert gardens, in California, the California buckeye (*Aesculus californica*), at fifteen to forty feet; the California juniper (*Juniperus californica*), at thirty feet; or the Coulter pine (*Pinus coulteri*), at forty to seventy feet, may form the canopy layer.

In Southern California, the lemonade berry (*Rhus integrifolia*) is highly regarded by some native plant experts. Various gooseberries are also native to the Sunshine State; check with the California Native Plant Society to see which might be most appropriate for your area. The snowdrop bush (*Styrax officinalis* var. *californica*) is recommended for drier gardens.

The ponderosa pine (*Pinus ponderosa*), which grows at higher elevations (7,000 feet or more) in the desert Southwest, is also found in eastern Washington at 2,500 feet. It can reach 60 to 130 feet in the wild.

A gardener can often have the most fun with the ground layer. Here you can plant the perennials and annuals you admire—always keeping in mind, of course, that the ultimate purpose is not only to please yourself and your family but also to feed and shelter the nonhuman creatures you're offering to share your space with. Every area in the nation has a multitude of native flowers to grow. After all, the New World started the gardening craze in England as settlers reported on the wonderfully beautiful plants they found here and plant hunters such as John Bartram and David Douglas sent back specimens. However, just because a book lists certain plants as native, don't rely on them for your area. The much-prized blue spruce is native to the United States, but in the wild it is found in the Colorado Rockies and requires a deep winter freeze to be happy and healthy. Your native plant society can tell you about specific plants found in your area.

The Design Process

Now that you have some background in the wildlife garden aesthetic and the use of native plants, you should understand the following pages on the design process. The garden plans on the next three pages, for a rectangular suburban lot, a small city lot, and for a balcony, lanai, or other small space, illustrate how you might translate plant communities in your area into a garden plan for your own space. I haven't assigned sizes to these plans, so you can adjust them to fit the space you have. But in general, the suburban lot might be roughly 100 feet by 100 feet, or any other squarish area. The small city lot might be thirty feet by fifty feet, and the balcony plan assumes an area about six feet by twelve feet.

Some books will tell you how to design a garden as if it would be finished once you or a landscape designer drew a plan and put in the plants. We've found that design is a continual process, and even after fifteen years, our garden is still not "finished." The plants themselves create changes or make changes necessary after we think the garden is complete.

By trial and error, and by reading and taking classes, I've discovered a process that I recommend, because it worked for us or because we should have done it this way. We began by getting to know our lot. After we had learned some things about it and had decided where we wanted open space and what sort of water garden we wanted and where we wanted the open spaces, we had a plan drawn by a professional designer to our specifications.

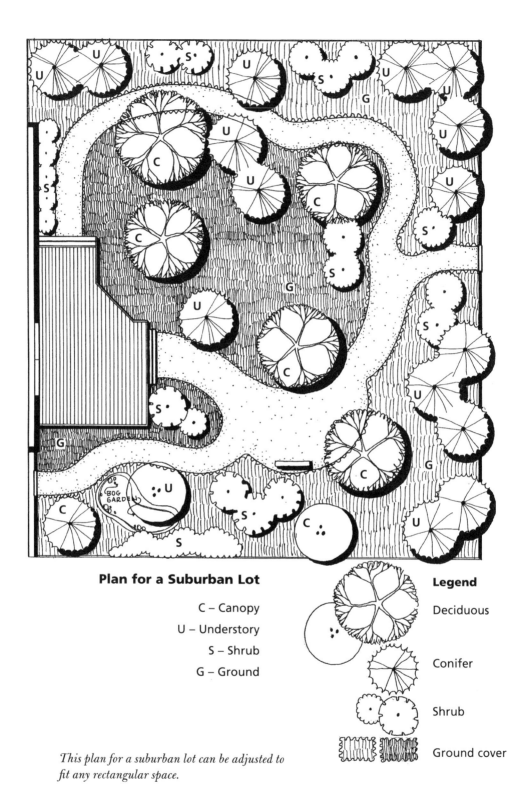

Plan for a Suburban Lot

C – Canopy
U – Understory
S – Shrub
G – Ground

Legend

Deciduous

Conifer

Shrub

Ground cover

This plan for a suburban lot can be adjusted to fit any rectangular space.

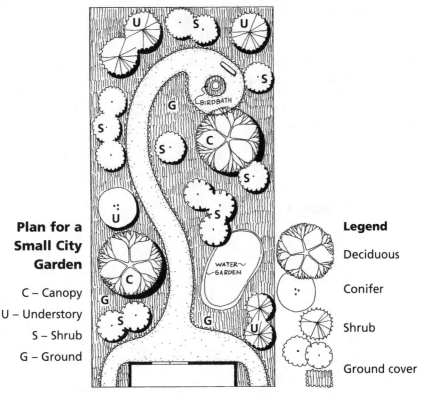

Plan for a Small City Garden

C – Canopy
U – Understory
S – Shrub
G – Ground

BIRDBATH

WATER~GARDEN

Legend

Deciduous

Conifer

Shrub

Ground cover

Even a small city garden can provide sanctuary for you and wildlife.

Of course, we made some mistakes. For example, instead of accepting the designer's recommendation that sweet woodruff made a good ground cover, I ought to have investigated more. I might have found out that, once planted, it's impossible to get rid of; it probably crowds out native ground covers that I'd like to encourage, and in the winter it looks ratty. Unfortunately, I still have a tendency to plant first and ask later.

We have learned that some tasks are best done before others—or along with others. Here, in general, are the steps as we've discovered them:

1. Get to know your space.
2. Understand what you need from the garden.
3. Lay out the spaces.
4. Draw a plan.
5. Lay the foundation.
6. Put in the plants.

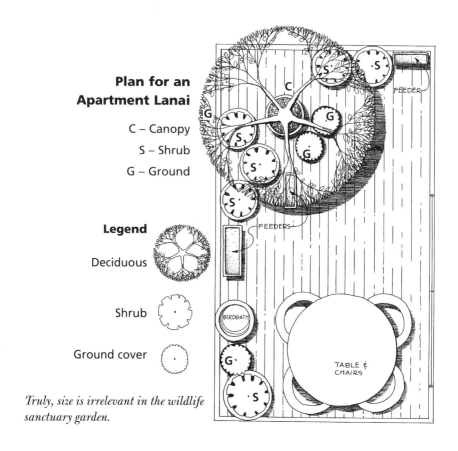

Plan for an Apartment Lanai

C – Canopy
S – Shrub
G – Ground

Legend

Deciduous

Shrub

Ground cover

FEEDER

C

G

S

S

G

S

G

S

FEEDERS

S

BIRDBATH

G

TABLE & CHAIRS

G

S

Truly, size is irrelevant in the wildlife sanctuary garden.

Get to Know Your Space

Landscape architects call this phase *site analysis*. No matter what size space you have to work with, you can provide the needed elements for wildlife—food, shelter, and water—and still have enough left over for you and your family. Get acquainted with the space you have, whether it's a large suburban lot, a small city garden, or an apartment dweller's lanai. The smaller the space, of course, the more limited the number of feeders you can provide or plants you can have, and consequently you will attract fewer species. Still, all of these elements can be present. Keep in mind that anything you do is better than nothing.

If you're working with a balcony or lanai, think about how many pots (for plants and water) it could support and how they might comfortably fit. Add chairs and a table for you and your loved ones. How structurally strong is the balcony? Is there a weight limit? How will you provide water for both potted plants and wildlife? How will you prevent water from leaking onto the furniture below? What pests might be attracted? Would rats be drawn to it? (City or Norway rats are not a species of wildlife. They came with Europeans and are found only with people.) If you intend to try a wildlife garden on a fire escape landing, find out what laws apply. You wouldn't want to put anything in the way of people fleeing from a fire.

If you're working with a city or suburban lot, consider what is there already. Some wild creature may have grown dependent on the rose hips, the nectar, or the seeds.

We all live with other people around us. Consider what covenants your neighborhood has. Do they mandate a similar appearance in front? How much of your front yard could you devote to the garden without upsetting the people around you? Maybe you can make friends for your garden by giving away plants to the neighbors. Plants reproduce themselves gladly, so I always have plenty of plants to give to anyone who expresses an interest in gardening. Fortunately, pretty flowers attract both wildlife and people.

Another recommendation is to put a border around your property. This can be as simple as edging a bed with rocks or putting up a fence. Our covenants forbid fencing in front of the house, but we put up a six-foot cedar fence around the rest of the lot. Robert Frost isn't the only one to notice that good fences make good neighbors.

Consider your climate. It's probably not enough to say you live in USDA zone eight or zone five. USDA hardiness zones, which wrap around the country from coast to coast, are based only on the average minimum temperatures per year. Atlanta and Seattle are both in zone eight, for example, but the climate of Atlanta is far different from that of Seattle. Atlanta is more humid, and it rains there in the summer. Seattle's humidity is around sixty-five percent most of the year, but just over thirty percent in the summer, during its annual drought. The last killing frost in the South normally occurs around April 10; in western Washington, it may not be safe to plant vegetables before May 1. Even then, the best barometer for planting is soil temperature; when the soil warms up to the touch, we can plant tomatoes. The growing season is 220 days in the South; here it's 150 to 190 days. Inland, in New England, and in the high desert Southwest, the growing season is ninety days.

In northern Alabama, outdoor work stops when it rains; here, the saying is, "If you don't do it in the rain, you don't do it."

Understand your microclimate, the angles of the sun, the direction of prevailing winds, the amounts of rainfall. Consider the angle of the sun and the amount of sun over the seasons in your area. How many sunny days do you normally have? If you want water lilies, how many hours of sunlight can you count on each day? (The recommendation for water lilies is six hours of full sun daily.) How many overcast days? UV rays penetrate clouds, but the cloud cover deepens the shade for your plants. How intense is the sun? What is your altitude?

Feel the wind. Let it ruffle your hair. What direction does it come from? How many inches of rainfall do you receive each year? When does it rain? How does it rain, in bursts, or a steady drizzle day after day? How much snow falls? How long does it stay?

How cold will your space be in the winter? Will icy winds howl around the balcony? Balconies are colder than the ground for the same reason bridges have more ice than roads; the wind can chill them from below. The soil in pots will probably freeze if you live where winters are cold and long. Can you bring the pots inside? Or will you have to start over every spring? If so, you may want to consider annuals rather than native perennials to feed pollinators and birds. What will happen to creatures in the winter time? Birds that overwinter, i.e., remain all year, in your area will need water and grit, especially when the snow flies. Lacking teeth, they need the grit to grind up their food with their gizzards.

Look at the ground. What's the soil like? Perhaps over time it has been altered by previous owners so that native plants might not grow in it. If it's a new home, the builders may have scraped away topsoil to prepare the building site; subsoil has no nutrients. Have it tested or buy an inexpensive soil test kit and test it yourself. If a native plant can't feed off the nutrients in the soil, it will die. There's no point in buying plants two or three times. That's discouraging and expensive. Your county extension office can provide information on soils, soil testing, and soil amendments. Look it up in the phone book among your county offices or on the Internet.

Look around you. Look at the local landscape or find some if you live in a city, and feel what it is telling you. Take a walk where the local plant life is relatively undisturbed, if possible. The local arboretum or botanical garden is a great place to learn about plants, and many of them have native plant sections. At these gardens, apartment dwellers can discover what native plants will thrive in pots.

There you can learn about the natural landscape buried under concrete and lawn. An arboretum is also a great place for city people to refresh spirits jaded by the jangle of car horns, sirens, the boom box next door, and laughter on a summer night. Los Angeles and its suburbs sprawl across a desert. To see what miracles of garden design can be made from desert plants, visit the desert garden at the Huntington or the Rancho Santa Ana Botanical Garden in Claremont, California (see Plate 1, following page 36). Among granite rocks speckled gray with mica that glints in the sun, the RASBG has planted beaver tail (*Opuntia basilaris*), a purplish green cactus, and desert lavender (*Hyptis emoryi*), a scented member of the mint family (Lamiaceae). The colors are subtle shades of pale blue-gray fading to white, and the desert lavender lightly perfumes the air (see Plate 2, following page 36).

Understand What You Need from the Garden

As you think about your space, make a wish list. This will help you understand what you need from your garden.

What do you want the garden to do for you? Consider what role it can play in your life and in the lives of your family members. It can soothe your spirits (see Plate 3, following page 36). It can educate you and your children. Anyone, adult or child, who likes to learn will have no end of fun in it.

It's hard to equal the fascination of watching life take place in a backyard sanctuary garden. A dozen chickadees, sparrows, and house wrens will gather on our platform feeder, and soon one of them will decide it owns the whole thing. Then the one little bird keeps so busy fighting off the others it gets hardly anything to eat. It's so busy defending its territory that soon someone is able to sneak in behind it and eat. Then another copies that one brave bird. Eventually, of course, the aggressive bird is defeated by sheer numbers and has to give up the battle. It flies to a nearby twig and sulks. If birds could pout, it would.

From what we've observed, the ingenuity of squirrels is boundless when it comes to gaining access to bird feeders. They seem to appreciate a challenge. They may keep the birds away for a while, but eventually the squirrels scurry off and the birds return.

Besides food and shelter, water is another essential ingredient for a backyard wildlife sanctuary. All animals need water, even in desert areas. The source can be small, a birdbath, or it can be a sizable pond. Westerners, even along the Northwest Coast, have to be careful about water, for the West is typically an arid region. If you have to be careful about water, you can put this resource to no better use than to enable other creatures to survive. To make up for using more water outside for animals, you might consider putting in drought-tolerant native plants, draining the swimming pool, or using less water inside the house.

Once established, a pond provides a great deal of enjoyment for everyone. The sound of running water soothes most people and lets everyone, human and nonhuman alike, know that there's water here. Birds come in and splash at the edges. Frogs establish themselves. Children love to see frogs or watch fish in a pond. Endlessly curious, children can always find something to see or do. The garden is ever changing and offering new experiences.

Even with all this, there can still be play spaces. If your family is sports-minded and you don't want to trek to a park or playground, put down "room to play ball" on the list. If you like golf and want to practice your putting, list that. If you have pets, consider their needs and balance that against the necessity to control them in the interests of wildlife.

When thinking of pets, consider how to control your own and other people's. This will help you solve problems before they emerge. A good fence, for example, can keep out the neighbor's large friendly dog (and keep yours in). When you make your plan, keep in mind the dog's pathways. If you preserve these, the dog's energetic romps will do much less damage. If yours is an outdoor dog—and all dogs are, at least partially— you might build a kennel as large as space allows and confine the dog there when you are not at home. Before our older dog died, he and the younger one, our two golden retrievers, were confined in their kennel while we were at work. When we were home, they had their own pathways through the garden, which they seldom deviated from. Consequently, when dogs are controlled, they do very little damage to the garden—or to its other inhabitants.

Is someone in your house a budding naturalist? Does that child bring home things that move on fewer than two legs or more than four? If so, what better place to release the creature than in your own garden. The child has the satisfaction of knowing the "pet" has a home, and you won't discover it when you go through the pockets on wash day. Ask the kids what they'd like. You may be surprised at the answers when they realize what the possibilities are.

If someone has physical limitations, think of how much that person can do and how to make it easier to get around. Being disabled need be no barrier to enjoying a garden or enjoying gardening, and considerable information is available on techniques people with disabilities can use to do some gardening. If someone has allergies, you can find out what plants cause, for example, hay fever, and avoid planting them.

Do you or others in your household hate gardening? Wildlife gardening has a big advantage in that, once it's established, the less attention you pay to it, the better for the wild creatures. Nature balances itself after a while; birds eat bugs that might devour plants. Our friends Judy and Mike have been turning their entire suburban yard into a wildlife garden. Mike hates mowing; Judy hates gardening. Because they want an attractive property that will be low maintenance, they use plants native to western Washington.

When thinking about everyone's activities, remember to save a space for relaxing and enjoying the garden, where you, your family, and your friends can cultivate the fine art of doing nothing.

Finally, prioritize everyone's wish list. Concentrate on the most important needs first, and scale down the lists from the dream to the possible, given your time, resources, and energy.

A wildlife garden "unites the human and the natural over time and change," says Roxanne Hamilton, professor of landscape architecture at the University of Washington. Gardens do change with the seasons, whatever the seasons are like in your area—subtle or dramatic. One of the great things about the wildlife sanctuary garden is the way it adapts to change of all sorts. Deciduous trees bud, leaf out, change color, shed their leaves, and go dormant. Flowers poke out of the ground, bud, bloom, set seed, and become dormant. They change from year to year, also. The canopy spreads out, and some understory trees become canopy trees. Wild visitors may come regularly for a few years, then disappear. New visitors will come by. We see a bird we don't recognize. A new plant appears, and I didn't plant it. There will always be a surprise.

Lay Out the Spaces

Before you draw a real plan, lay out the spaces of your garden. This will be a pretty rough sketch, maybe with colored markers on newsprint or tracing paper. The plan, as Wordsworth said, is your guide to the "invisible hand of art." Here you think in two dimensions: the flat spaces and the vertical tiers (canopy, understory, shrub, and ground). Putting it on paper helps you to think through the design, even if, like me, you can't draw. Initially, you don't have to do anything but roughly represent the spaces. Landscape architects call this the *base map*.

As you proceed, keep in mind the needs of the wildlife you are hoping to attract. As much as possible, retain large areas as undisturbed ground for sheltering, nesting, and traveling. Wild creatures need a means to get around, too! Put play areas and other busy places close together in the center of the garden to reduce the impact on wildlife. Keep existing trees as much as possible.

Think of the vantage points. Wildlife doesn't come unless the animals think they're alone, so place feeders and water sources where you can see the animals and enjoy their behavior without them seeing you. If necessary, you might want to consider building a blind outdoors. A blind is a type of screen through which you can watch the animals without disturbing them. (If you like photographing wildlife, you might need a 200 mm lens.) Our house functions as a blind of sorts. From most of the windows we can watch the creatures, but they can't see us. If you don't have a blind, some animals will resume their activities after you have sat quite still for fifteen minutes to half an hour.

When you lay out the spaces, begin from your access points. These are the points from which you will enter and leave the garden. We have

Plate 1. *This California fan palm grows at the Rancho Santa Ana Botanical Garden in Claremont, California.*

Plate 2. Desert plants have a subtle, architectural beauty.

Plate 3. This small trail in a garden invites us to a contemplative bench.

two access points, one is a gate and the other is our back door. These allow us to go and come with minimal impact on the wildlife. Work from the outermost perimeter of your space inward in a series of rings or borders. First is the outermost border, in our case, along the fence and property line. Next come one or two transition borders, and closest in are the people areas.

Let the outer border be as wild as it can be. Here the critters will nest and take shelter, as far as possible from the human activity in the center areas. Here, you plant the canopy layer; the bigger trees that will stand at the perimeter, intermingled with understory trees. If you don't have space for canopy trees, use understory trees as the top tier, but be careful to plant trees that can take full sun.

The next ring is the understory or shrub layer, depending on whether you have space for four or three tiers. It might be semi-wild, with a mixture of compatible exotics and native plants.

In the third ring, plant perennials and small shrubs. These rings make a transition between the wild areas, for creatures, and the center, for people.

The center is yours. Here you plant your lawn or put in a patio. The only consideration is to manage "your" spaces so as to have the least impact possible on surrounding natives. If you have a lawn, remember that lawns typically need a sweeter, or more basic, soil. If the native soil in your area is acidic (has a pH number below seven), you will have to add lime to sweeten the soil. If you decide a lawn is worth the work and possible damage to acid-loving native plants at the perimeters, use organic methods to care for it. (Your county extension office or master gardener program can tell you which grasses make the best lawns and how to care for lawns in your area.) Mow the lawn with a push or electric mower to minimize the noise and be less frightening to wildlife.

Referring to our garden plan, notice that at the outer border we have planted a mix of evergreens and deciduous trees. Our lot is not large enough for a pure canopy layer followed by an understory layer. We have mixed smaller (fifteen to twenty-five foot) understory trees with the Douglas fir and bigleaf maple canopy in the same outer border. The smaller trees include flowering trees with red foliage, hinoki cypress, Engelmann spruce, and Japanese black pine.

In front of this outer ring, the transition border forms the shrub layer. Because we don't have room for large numbers of perennials, we have planted mostly flowering shrubs: dogwood and rhododendrons, weigela and spirea, *Osmanthus delavayi*. This mixture of exotic and native flowering shrubs is semi-wild. In front of these plants, and in some cases mixed in with them, are the perennials, primarily those that thrive in the shade: trillium, violets, astilbe, and bleeding hearts (both the large exotic and small native).

The inner spaces belong to us. We have a large graveled "patio" with a small table and chairs made of plantation teak. These are weathering into a pretty silver. They are placed to allow us to sit and look at the upper pond, which lies at the foot of the larger patio. The second, smaller patio is at the south side of the house. Here, even though the area is only ten feet wide at its widest, we are able to keep to the pattern by using the Japanese idea of "borrowing" from an adjacent or distant land-scape. In this case, the canopy trees are on the neighbor's property: a bigleaf maple and a row of young Douglas firs along the fence. The understory tree is a Japanese snowbell, interplanted with flowering shrubs—rhododendrons and azaleas. The trilliums grow in the shadowy places, and the hardy cyclamen in part shade and sun.

Behind the house, at the farthest corner, is the dog kennel, shaded by a bigleaf maple and a flowering plum. Between the house and the kennel, we have left the area wild, except for putting in two witch hazels and a dogwood shrub. Here the bigger cascara hums with bees in the spring, and the red huckleberry puts out fruit for happy birds.

When you determine the shape of your garden spaces, think about the natural world. First, there are no straight lines in nature. The British artist William Hogarth was the first to insist on this idea, back in the middle of the eighteenth century. His idea led the landscape designer Lancelot "Capability" Brown to seize on the idea of the **S** as the ideal beautiful line, which could be used to improve-upon nature. He "improved" large estates, such as Blenheim Palace, by making the grounds into grassy parks with curving lines of woods and streams, and clumps of trees placed here and there on the acres of lawns. From our perspective, Brown carried his idea too far; he destroyed more than a few natural streams to make them flow in gentle, undulating curves. At the beginning of the nineteenth century, Wordsworth was grumbling out loud and in letters to friends about the idea of improving on nature, the idea that people could make nature more beautiful than it was. The streams in his gardens still tumble down the hillsides of the English Lake District.

Second, nature does not provide rooms, so the popular concept of garden rooms is out of step with nature. Yet people are happier with defined spaces. By way of compromise, our garden plan lets the spaces flow around the house. Pathways curve, and the open areas (what we call "patios") are rounded. Flowing, curved lines are more comfortable than straight lines and square corners for most creatures, including us.

If you are planning to turn your balcony into a wildlife sanctuary, obviously, you would not want to grow a sequoia for a canopy tree, but think of the layers in terms of what can be grown in pots. If possible, try to have at least one "canopy" tree that can tolerate full sun and drying winds, or any other adverse conditions you identified in getting acquainted with the space. This tree will shade the other plants and may provide food and shelter for birds. It might be a dwarf conifer or a dwarf cherry.

If large trees are already on your property and nothing can change your mind about shortening them, do not top them. Topping means to cut off the top twenty or thirty feet of the tree. (Unfortunately, it's a common practice here among developers, people who are afraid of windstorms damaging their houses, and people who want a view.) This ensures a slow death for the tree and problems for you. After a few years, the trees will split from the top, and the branches that suckered from the tall stumps will break off and cause almost as much damage as they would have if left alone.

A big tree will die more quickly if you cut it back to about twenty feet. It will form a snag, a dead tree riddled by bugs, which will provide food for woodpeckers and holes for cavity-nesting birds. By cutting large trees, however, you will miss out on the fun of attracting birds that nest high. I was delighted one afternoon in late March by the dance of the northern flickers (large woodpeckers) along the bare high branches of the bigleaf maples. Back and forth, chucking and calling, they danced. In the sunshine and crisp air, this high-stepping ballet made me happy and gives me joy to remember.

Draw a Plan

Having laid out the spaces in your base map, you can proceed now to make it a bit more detailed. After you sketch out your borders, lay a piece of tracing paper over the base map and sketch in the items on everyone's wish lists. Landscape architects call this the *bubble diagram,* because it puts circles around general areas rather than drawing specific features in detail. For example, you might draw in a play area for children and an observation area for watching birds at the feeders. When showing view areas, remember to think about what you'll see from inside the house, from a porch or deck, or from a patio.

In this phase you and your family might talk over the items on everyone's wish lists and decide where each should go. You might set aside a place for the compost pile in a screened utility area, because it may not be the handsomest item in your garden. You could place a water garden in the middle of an open space to function both as the garden's centerpiece and to provide moisture to the greater number of plants around it. (It will humidify the garden and decrease the amount of watering you have to do.)

Plot out the functional areas: for play, for the vegetable garden, or for your favorite flowers. You might have different functional areas for different animals you want to attract: a butterfly garden or a garden for bees. Draw the permanent existing features in their locations: the property lines, the house, driveway, walks. Follow the conventions of any map-maker, putting north at the top. This will serve as a constant reminder of where the sun shines on the property and where the property is shady.

For a balcony, draw the location of the door into the apartment, and a fire escape if there is one connected to it. Try to draw the existing conditions as accurately as you can. Put in the dimensions of the house and other buildings, and as nearly as possible the spread of trees. You can use a magic marker in a color that will show through several layers of tracing paper as you go through the next steps.

Consider your neighbors' sensibilities. The object of your garden is not only to attract wildlife but other people to the idea of a wildlife sanctuary garden. To avoid contention and make your garden appealing to your neighbors, put a border around it. Because we put a fence around the property, we have never had a complaint about what we're doing with our garden or why we don't have a lawn. My friend Judy's neighbors looked askance at the work she was doing in a bed in front of her house until she edged it with stones salvaged from digging. Then they complimented her on how much better the bed looked.

If you have covenants in your community that require certain standards for the front of your property, follow them. We have been fortunate in that our lot actually lies behind another one, so we screened our front yard from the neighbor's backyard by planting Portugal laurels. That screening enabled us to include the front in the wildlife garden without offending anyone. If your covenants require a setback with lawn (a set amount of space between the street and your house), you might make islands of native plantings and put in birdbaths. I've seen quite an expensive house with a dead tree in the front. The homeowners have shown great ingenuity in planting trees to screen it and curving their driveway around it. Another homeowner gradually widened the islands and borders so that the front lawn now occupies considerably less area than it did. A third homeowner angled the walkway to the front door and lined it with plantings on one side. On the side between the driveway and the walk, they put in plants only. All of these solutions have been so tastefully done that it would be difficult for anyone to object, and I assume no one has objected, because these yards have all been in existence for several years.

If you're as shy about drawing as I am, there are tools available for drawing garden plans. Landscape and garden design software exists for the home computer, if you have one. If you're not comfortable with a computer, you can find paper packages with templates for various types and sizes of plants, along with graph paper. Your county extension office may have a package you can purchase for a reasonable cost. If there are professional landscape designers in your area, you might call on one to make the plan for you, to be certain the plan is to scale. To find a reputable designer, call the nearest college or university and ask if they have a school of landscape architecture. An advanced student or member of the faculty may be available to help. Not everyone calling himself a landscape or garden designer really is one, so in your own interests ask for their credentials.

Another way to have a plan drawn, depending on the size of your space, might be to lay out the spaces with string and stakes. This might work best where the lot is mostly lawn and you intend to reclaim all or a portion of it for your sanctuary. You can see where the spaces will be and how the paths will connect them. This method is often recommended for laying out a pond in a lawn, because people can see the shape of the pond and its placement relative to the rest of the space.

After you have decided on the features of your garden, for human and nonhuman inhabitants alike, draw a detailed plan. Make it as final as you can, but plan on changing it over time. The area you intend for dry perennials may turn out to be a bog garden. Slugs may devour your bee balm, a windstorm might break a high branch and leave that shady area bare and sunny. You might plant a recommended native berry plant and find that it's so invasive it threatens to take over the world. As time goes on, the canopy trees will provide more shade.

Be prepared to find that the best plans are those you can change when you want to. Not the least of the changes will be your own, especially if you like to experiment with plants and can't resist tinkering with the planting design as time goes on. Dick jokes that the motto of our garden is, "Have roots, will travel."

Lay the Foundation

The design of our garden has a strong structural base of curving gravel pathways and graveled open spaces edged in mossy brick. We hadn't originally planned to use brick, but we needed a way to clearly define the spaces and pathways. At first we used bender board, strips of thin wood about six inches wide and twelve feet long. It was inexpensive, but unfortunately, it rotted and broke easily. So we decided on brick.

The first step in laying the garden foundation was to lay the brick edging. To do that, we outlined the edges with string. Next, we dug a trench along the string. Then we mortared in the bricks and let the mortar dry. Fifteen years later, the brick edging holds the garden in place. In the beginning, the brick was not exactly "invisible," as in Wordsworth's law of garden design, but over time natural moss has softened the look of the bricks. Plants sprawl over the bricks in some areas too, enough to contribute to the softening effect but not enough to lose the structure.

The patios and pathways around the house and the water garden are gravel. We laid crushed gravel over a fabric liner that lets water through and prevents deep-rooted weeds from coming up. We keep weeds out of the gravel for the most part, but we don't use chemical herbicides, because they might make birds sick or imperil tree roots.

We have seen gardens in which the open areas were pea gravel, but they were hard to walk in. Other gardens that did not use a fabric layer found the gravel disappearing into mud during the winter. The fabric and gravel in our garden have remained firm underfoot.

Put in the Plants

Is there anything as enjoyable to a gardener as tracking down the right plant or discovering a new one to try out? In the Seattle area, I can go to a nursery, buy a latte, and sip while I browse happily among the plants.

When considering your plantings, find out what the soil type and pH of the soil are. Because the soil might have been mistreated by previous owners or by the builders, you may find yourself wanting to return the soil to a previous condition. It's not uncommon for some gardeners to spend three or more years amending the soil so they can grow the right plants for the wildlife they want to attract. Your county extension service can advise you on what's right for your area, or you might check with the local native plant society. Once you have the right soil for what you want to do, select plants that thrive in those conditions.

Plant the canopy layer first, followed by the understory, the shrub layer, and the ground layer, in that order. Try to realize that plants get bigger. From time to time I have to find new homes for plants that have been crowded out of their original places.

When choosing plants, whenever possible select native plants over exotics, because these plants carry food recognizable to indigenous wildlife.

If you garden with a mixture of exotics and native plants, as I do, try to limit your garden palette to those exotics that are compatible with the conditions, soil type, and pH of your area. A combination of natives and compatible exotics that has worked well in our garden is composed of a Nootka rose (*Rosa nutkana*) that is native to Nootka Island in British Columbia, salal (a native ground cover), a shrub dogwood (the native *Cornus sericea*), and a species rhododendron (*Rhododendron strigillosum*). These plants have the same basic cultural requirements, and rhododendrons especially are satisfied to grow with other plants. Gardeners refer to them as "sociable plants," which conjures up pictures of rhodies having the other garden denizens over for tea.

These plants all need acidic soils and can tolerate moist cloudy days and damp soil in the wintertime. All of them do well as understory shrubs in the shade of the bigleaf maples and Douglas firs that stand at the outer rim of the garden. Rhododendrons, however, must have occasional water during the summer drought.

Try to investigate before you use exotics because some may be detrimental to native plant populations. Birds and other animals can carry seeds into natural areas, which may then be overrun with the exotic. Himalayan blackberries, for instance, are a problem in Pacific Northwest forests, as are hollies and herb Robert.

If you have the space, you might imitate a portion of the natural landscape: a mini desert, a small woodland, a bit of prairie, or a wetland. These can form the basis of your garden, or you might devote a portion of your area to one of these themes.

If you live in an apartment or condominium, consider your lanai as a climate zone separate from the USDA climate zone you live in. If the lanai is off the ground, it will be colder in winter than the ground. Also take into consideration the amount and direction of sunlight, the summer temperatures, and the need for water. Provide animals with shade; in the desert Southwest, a large cactus or two could be welcome shade features that endure the heat of the day. Try to use native plants that can survive where you plant them.

For the rest, let things happen. We let plants seed themselves where they will and only pull out the ones that would interfere with the sprinkler system or other plants. Wildflowers that seed themselves here aren't weeds by definition, only by performance—if they are in the wrong place or are a pest plant (see chapter 6).

Sometimes we have help with planting from the garden's other occupants. One day when I was reading in the garden, I heard the skittering of small paws and looked up to see a squirrel running along the fence. It ran over to a hosta and dug a small hole beside it. Into this hole, the squirrel dropped something, then carefully covered it over with dirt. Still not content, it bent one of the large hosta leaves down and patted it over the place. The next year, a hardy cyclamen grew next to the hosta. I hadn't thought of combining hostas with cyclamen, but I couldn't overlook a good idea, even from a squirrel, so I planted some more.

We feed the squirrels corn, and everywhere at the end of summer I find corn seedlings sprouting—even in the ornamental containers near the front porch. I liked the look of these small plants, with their gracefully arching leaves, in contrast to the trailing carnations and miniature

Sometimes, as in this plant combination courtesy of a squirrel, nature provides happy surprises.

box in the pots. And in the microclimate of this garden, I have no fear that they will ever be as "high as an elephant's eye."

Let It Grow

A wildlife garden design begins with your decision to share your space with wildlife and continues through the design process. As you plant and take delight in the growing, living plants and animals, you will begin to notice that other factors influence the design. Squirrel plantings are just an example. Wonderful things will happen in the garden if you let them. Wait and see.

Chapter 3

Gardening with Native Plants

A native plant is one that grew in a particular area before European settlers arrived, bringing with them their favorites from the old country. An exotic is a plant that came from somewhere else: Europe, Asia, or another part of the United States. Some garden catalogs advertise plants as native if they originate in the United States, Mexico, or Canada, but it's important to understand that a native plant should mean native to your area. Some books suggest that you should consider plants native only if they grow or grew within a radius of fifty miles from your home. However, considering the widely divergent microclimates in a much smaller area, that range might be much smaller. Plant communities develop differently on a sunny slope than on a shady one. Altitude makes a difference too, as do climate and soil. Before I understood this, I wanted a tree with the strong structure of a spruce. The Engelmann spruce (*Picea engelmanii*) is native to Washington State, while the beautiful high-altitude Colorado blue spruce would have a difficult time at sea level, without the deep winter chill it has adapted to. I bought and planted an Engelmann spruce. Later, I realized that it might not thrive because it is native to eastern Washington, where the climate is much drier (only nine inches of annual moisture) and the soils are alkaline rather than acidic. So far, after five years, it's doing OK, but I wonder how much better it might do in its proper place.

In the wildlife garden, if you grow nonnative plants, wild creatures may not recognize them as sources of food and could literally go hungry in a garden of plenty. On the other hand, I don't advocate being a purist and growing only native plants, if you have some exotic favorites. The animals aren't the only ones to benefit from the garden, after all. If you do wish to grow exotic plants as well as natives, you'll have much less work, and the plants will do better, if you grow compatible exotics.

Compatible exotics are those that originated elsewhere but thrive in conditions similar to those found in your garden. Horticulturally speaking, their cultural needs are similar. (A plant's "cultural" needs are those conditions—climate, soil, nutrients, and moisture—that it must have in order to thrive or even survive.) An exotic plant will be compatible with natives when your garden microclimate contains the moisture, soil type, soil acidity, sunlight, and humidity that it requires.

For example, I can't resist growing peonies. I inherited a wonderful Edulis Superba with petals that are pink with white edges, that is now nearly eighty years old. Loving it, I acquired five others, including a tree peony. All of these are exotic hybrids whose forebears originated in China. Although they require a soil pH that is neutral to acid, i.e., about 6 to 9 on the 14-point scale, they grow well with rhododendrons and the native acid lovers, whose preference is about 4.5 to 6 on the same scale. Our soil pH is around six, so the range for all of these types of plants overlaps. Peonies are hospitable to ants, who eat aphids, and bees seem to like their nectar.

Western Washington's soil is primarily acidic, so rhododendrons and heathers, which thrive on acidic soils, do well here, along with our acid-loving natives. Various species of artemisia or sage do well in eastern Washington, although they aren't native there, because they thrive in alkaline soils. The photo on the next page shows a grouping of native desert plants in the whitish alkaline soil of eastern Washington.

As you can tell from the discussion above, I think compatible exotics have a place in the wildlife garden. They are resistant to pests like the native plants, and they attract similar species of wild creatures. If the exotics are also beautiful, they have a place in the garden. For example,

These desert plants in eastern Washington have formed a community, which is also a pleasing arrangement of plant material.

Rhododendron macrophyllum, the Washington state flower, is native to the western slope of the Cascade Mountains in Washington and Oregon. Hybrid rhododendrons are a gardening staple of the area around Puget Sound and make bumblebees very happy while they're in bloom. When they're not in bloom, their evergreen leaves add to the texture of greens in the garden, and they are beautiful in our clammy winters. One local wildlife gardener in a warmer part of the area grows very early flowering *R. dauricum* and one of its hybrids *R. d.* "Midwinter" to attract Anna's hummingbirds during December and January. Neither of these is native to the contiguous United States.

Hummingbirds in our garden feast on both the native honeysuckle (*Lonicera ciliosa*) and a hybrid honeysuckle. Both have the long, trumpet-shaped flowers that are ideal for attracting and feeding hummingbirds, who can insert their bills deep into them. I haven't seen a bird or a bee around the winter-flowering *L. fragrantissima,* but I certainly appreciate its yellow flowers and its scent, even when it is capped with snow.

In February, blooms from the exotic *Pieris japonica* shrub at our front door attract bumblebees. Not only are bumblebees not supposed to be able to fly (according to the laws of aerodynamics), they certainly aren't supposed to fly in February. But they do.

Even if you can't re-create the ecosystem of the original vegetation, you can think in terms of plant groupings and include both native plants and compatible exotics. Plate 4 (following page 68) shows our front yard in the winter of 1995–1996, the year after we put in plugs of Irish moss as a simulated "lawn." To the left, the green leaves are those of the laurels that screen the house from the neighbor's backyard. The tall, columnar trunks rising from the center background belong to a bigleaf maple, as does the trunk at the right, behind the young Douglas fir. Between the two canopy trees, and in front of the "Doug fir," is an original native plant grouping. Growing from the stump of a western red cedar is another one, together with a western red huckleberry. At the base of the shrub are native sword ferns (*Polystichum munitum*) intermingled with heather in bloom.

I realize that advocating growing exotics in a native garden is controversial in some circles. There's a wide range of opinion on this subject, with some people insisting that you shouldn't plant anything that did not grow in the original plant community of your area. This proscription would include some exotics that are recommended because they attract bees, butterflies, and birds. As you can see from Plate 5 (following page 68), these asters, although not native to this area, make bees happy late in the summer.

Another factor in deciding what exotics to plant in your garden is the possibility of damaging natural areas. Some plants, such as herb Robert or holly, are invasive and can cause damage to West Coast forests. In the South, water hyacinth is banned because it can choke waterways. Purple loosestrife is banned nearly everywhere for the same reason. Recently, yellow flag iris (*Iris pseudacorus*) has appeared on some lists of plants to watch because it too proliferates in water.

While responsible wildlife gardeners investigate to be sure they're not planting something that could harm wildlife outside the garden, there is a place for exotics in the wildlife sanctuary garden. When deciding how far to restore the original natural surroundings where you live, or what exotics to include, consider what is right to do and then apply your own native common sense.

Some people insist that it may be neither possible nor right to restore the original ecosystems, particularly in cities where the ecology has been so altered that the original plant communities would not survive. In these paved places, plants have to be tough. Cities are warmer than the surrounding countryside because they have fewer trees and other vegetation to cool off the concrete that absorbs heat. They are also drier because there are fewer plants to add moisture to the air through their transpiration.

Obviously, in a balcony or small patio garden, it's impossible to re-create or imitate a forest or a prairie. You may want to take a different approach. You might consider which plants are the best for your balcony microclimates, as you learned in chapter 2, or you can grow plants that appeal to local pollinators and birds.

In northern cities, the urban climate would be warmer and drier than originally, but in southern cities, it might be cooler, particularly in the desert Southwest, where people grow lawns. Watering lawns adds artificial moisture to the air. In these areas, your local native plant society or chapter of the Audubon Society can help you with your selection. It may be that certain exotics are most likely to attract local birds and pollinators.

Along with growing plants to attract birds and bees, you can provide continuous water, for which they will be most grateful during hot, dry summers or icy winters. In northern cities, a hospitable balcony may save birds from starvation or from freezing to death or dying of thirst because other water sources are frozen over.

Acquiring Native Plants

It is sensible and fashionable these days to garden with native plants. They are so popular in some areas of the country that some people gather them from the wild and, in so doing, destroy or damage the plant communities the plants once contributed to. A plant's loss affects the relationship of the various plants in its plant community, and the animals that depended on that plant for food won't be able to find it. For this reason, the Forest Service forbids gathering wild plants, except with a permit to do so in specific areas, such as under a power line.

Buying native plants can also be hazardous to plant communities, if we don't know where the plant originated. Some nurseries are not above buying plants from people who gather them from the wild. Nursery-propagated native plants are not yet common in the marketplace—at least not around here. When they are, it will be immensely beneficial to the natural world. In the meantime, we have to be certain that our purchases are made with the larger world in mind.

When you buy a plant, look for a certificate of its origin. This certificate should promise you that the plant was rescued from development or taken from private property (such as another wildlife sanctuary garden) with the permission of the owner. If it was collected from the wild, there should be a statement certifying that the collector had permission from the U.S. Forest Service or from the property owner. The Forest Service is (or should be) the guardian of our public lands. On land controlled by the U.S. Forest Service, be sure to contact your local ranger station to get a permit to collect a plant. This may entail a somewhat lengthy permit process, but it's worth it to know you're doing the right thing. If a plant is gathered from private property without permission of the owner, it is theft, even if the land is scheduled for development. If there is no certificate and the nursery can't tell you how a plant was gathered, don't buy it.

You don't have to feel that you must rescue a plant from a nursery whose ethics are in doubt. Your purchase will only encourage unscrupulous people to engage in more theft from natural areas. If you happen upon a plant in an area slated for development, resist the temptation to collect it until you ask the developer for permission.

Occasionally the developer may not be able to give you permission to gather or rescue a native plant, because of a contradiction in the laws. A member of the Wildlife Garden Forum on the Internet told of encountering a developer who said he couldn't give permission to take plants from land slated for development, because the laws forbade gathering on that land. Apparently, it could be developed, but plants couldn't be taken. Until the plants were destroyed by the bulldozer, they couldn't be gathered! It was a legal catch-22.

Be sure to check the legalities first. If you're unclear about what to do, ask your local or state native plant society. If you have access to the

Internet, consult the people in the Native Plant Forum. The URL is www.gardenweb.com/forums/natives. You might also consult the people in the Wildlife Garden Forum. The URL is www.nature.net/forums/garden.

If you come across a plant while out in the wild, leave it where you found it. You might remember its location and return when it is in seed. Collect seed only. Do some research about the plant. A plant may look delectable in the wild but be unable to survive in your garden.

Once native plants get going in your garden, you may not have to think about buying or collecting more of them. One of the adaptations native plants have made for their survival is prolific breeding. If they find your garden hospitable, you will have more of them. Pollinators will ensure that there is plenty of seed, and the wind and the animals will contribute to spreading the seed. Plants that spread by underground runners will pop up here and there. In time, you can maintain the design of the garden just by pulling plants out where you don't want them to be.

Should you want to propagate plants yourself, however, you can use the techniques employed for other garden plants. Sow seed, make divisions, and take cuttings.

Gardening with Plant Communities

Native plant communities are vital to making a wildlife sanctuary garden. Many species of insects and animals require specific types of vegetation to survive. But it's not always possible, especially if you're a city dweller, to limit your plant palette to those native plants that grew within a short radius of your location. (See the section "Native Plant Controversies" on page 67.) However, planting and encouraging native plant communities is necessary to having a true sanctuary garden, because you're not only providing space for wildlife but for wild plants as well. A native plant community is vital to developing a garden ecosystem. When you garden with plant communities, an ecosystem will evolve over time in your garden. Where hospitable plant communities exist as sources of food and shelter, and where there is a reliable source of water on the property or close by, animals will move in, and plants and animals will develop an interdependence.

Plant communities differ from one area to another. Only in parts of the Puget Sound area, for example, do beautiful flowering native madrona trees grow as understory trees beneath Douglas fir. In other parts of the area, these trees are not found naturally. Where they are not found naturally, you will have more trouble growing them.

Plants in a plant community are living organisms that go through the normal life cycle, including death. Even in death, the members of the community make their contribution to the living. Dead trees, or snags, for example, become hosts to insects such as beetles, whose larvae feed on the soft wood. In turn these creatures become food for woodpeckers and chickadees, who drill out holes in the snag to find them. Other animals—raccoons, squirrels, and owls—nest in these cavities. When you garden for wildlife, remember to include snags as well as live trees. Plate 6 (following page 68) shows a snag left as part of a plant community in a garden in the Puget Sound area. This snag is home to beetles and other insects that attract woodpeckers. It also serves as a striking design focal point.

When we moved onto our lot and began to make a garden, we began with some native plants that were already on the property. We added three Douglas firs that will eventually form the canopy layer along with the existing bigleaf maples. Now fifteen years old and approximately twenty-five feet tall, the Douglas firs form part of the upper understory layer, along with some spring-flowering cherry trees. The shrubs—red flowering currant, salmonberry, Nootka rose, elderberry, and Indian plum—can thrive in the shade of these larger trees. At the ground layer, the sword ferns, some three feet tall and five feet in diameter, accompany the salal, native bleeding heart, and trillium, along with other flowering perennials and some annuals. (Please refer to the plan of our garden on page 19.) Except for the peonies, most exotic plants are those recommended for wildlife by the Washington State Backyard Wildlife Sanctuary Program.

In addition, the water garden is home to fish, frogs, and a pair of ducks that visit every spring. (They might stay, except that we're about a block from a wetland.)

Re-creating the Ecosystem

The aim of wildlife gardening is to make our gardens look and act like our native landscapes. Because plant communities become habitats for animals, a healthy plant community is the first step in re-creating an ecosystem.

Here's how the ecosystem works in our garden. Soil microbes break down dead plant and animal matter until it is reduced to its essential chemicals and becomes part of the soil. These chemicals are the nutrients plants need for their health. Plants take up the chemicals through the cell walls of their roots, which travel upward through the plant and are transformed into growth. The soil microbes are also eaten by larger organisms, such as worms and burrowing insects, which themselves are dinner for birds and underground animals such as moles. Both plants and smaller animals become food for larger animals.

Here is a diagram of how nitrogen, an essential nutrient for plants, works its way through the food chain. The nitrogen cycle, somewhat like the food chain, shows who eats whom—or what.

Nitrogen Cycle

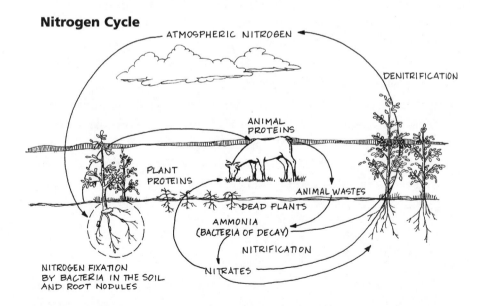

This illustration shows how nitrogen circulates in nature, in a continual cycle of nitrification and denitrification.

In a garden ecosystem, as in the larger ecosystem, life begins with death. Dead leaves and kitchen waste in our compost pile are reduced by the combined efforts of microbes, worms, and small insects. We incorporated some fallen logs originally on our property into the design of the garden. These provide food for microbes and insects, which have been busy breaking down the wood in the logs. Some types of insects eat the dead wood and are in turn eaten by other insects and by woodpeckers. In the soil, dead vegetable matter provides food for worms and larger organisms, which are in their turn eaten. Black beetles eat some bugs, which are also eaten by birds. Some birds munch on worms and ground-based insects. The northern flicker drills into fallen logs for its dinner; purple-and-green swallows swoop through the air gulping down flying insects. Hummingbirds feast on nectar from coral bells and honeysuckle, while bumblebees, honeybees, and native mason bees pollinate as they gather nectar from Japanese anemone, columbines, and other flowers.

In the winter, birds not only eat from the feeders, they lunch on the pyracantha berries. One late winter's day, robins and starlings, which had flocked together, descended on the pyracanthas and stripped them of their berries. In this garden, even slugs have their role. They are part of nature's cleanup crew. Not only do they clean up dog poop, they clean the rhododendrons of spent flower petals. In turn, they are food for the ducks who visit our water garden.

In our garden, it appears that, over the past decade and a half, compatible exotics and native plants have adapted to each other and formed an ecosystem.

Even if you can't recreate the ecosystem of the original vegetation, you can think in terms of plant communities and include both native plants and compatible exotics.

Selecting the Plants

To select the plants for your garden, work from the sky down. Begin with the tallest plants and work your way down to the ground layer. This might be the canopy layer or the understory layer, depending on the space you have available. Select the biggest native trees you can fit into the property. You might be able to find a dwarf hybrid of the native species and use it if space is limited, but keep in mind that *dwarf* is a relative term. A dwarf redwood would still be a very large tree. If you're planting a meadow, begin with the tallest grasses or wildflowers. If you're planting a wetland, start with the tallest emergent plants (see chapter 5). Under them, plant the next layer, and so on until you reach the ground.

To learn which plants would work best in your garden, consult a reputable native plant nursery or your local native plant society. They can both help in choosing the right plants. Or you might take a walk outdoors in a natural area as close to your home as you can get, and bring a notebook and a guidebook to local native plants. Jot down the names of plants you see and look for them in the nurseries.

Planting Native Plants

Success with native plants depends, to begin with, on carefully selecting the right plant for your garden's microclimate. You learned what's involved in this in chapter 2, when you read about learning to understand your space (the site analysis). The aim in building any sort of garden is to make a happy place. And as most of us know, happiness depends in some degree on the health of the organism. Keeping plants happy in any garden begins with their health, and a plant's health begins with the soil it grows in.

What Soil Is

Soil is made up of particles of sand, silt, clay, and humus. These particles vary in size from visible to microscopic; sand is the largest, silt is medium-sized, and clay is very fine. Soils that are too sandy will not hold moisture well. A clay soil will hold moisture too long and, in rainy climates, may tend to become waterlogged. Plants growing in clay may fall victim to the condition known as "wet feet" and rot away. (Unless they're bog plants or aquatics that need to have their roots constantly moist— but that's a subject for chapter 5.) A silty soil is not so heavy as clay, but it is slower to drain than sandy soils.

Silt, sand, and clay particles make up the soil's texture. The ideal soil texture varies with the purpose; the best soil for growing your lawn should be sandier, for better drainage, than garden soils. The best texture for garden soil is loamy. A mixture of sand, silt, and clay particles makes a loam.

Humus is the organic portion of soil. Some authorities recommend at least 4 percent humus. Humus can be made of decomposed kitchen vegetable scraps, ground-up leaves, worm castings, grass clippings, or other substances, except meat, in which flies breed maggots. One of the best sources of humus is compost. You can make compost in your own yard by putting kitchen scraps, grass clippings, and fallen leaves in a pile and letting them rot. All you have to do is to turn the compost pile now and then and make sure it doesn't dry out. Humus adds to the texture of the soil by making more surfaces for plant nutrients and water to adhere to. Adding humus is called *amending* the soil. Soil amendments do not add nutrients; they loosen clay or silty soils and hold water and nutrients in sandy soils. Once the humus is broken down to a dark, soil-like consistency, dig it into the soil.

How Soil Works

Soil, including its amendments, works to supply nutrients to plants by means of ions. Ions are atoms or groups of atoms that have an electric charge. Soil particles have a negative charge (–). Nutrient ions that have a positive charge (+) stick to these negatively charged soil particles. Plants take in nutrients by absorbing nutrient ions through the cell walls in their roots.

Of all the elements in the periodic table, only sixteen have been found to be necessary for plant life and growth. These are divided into categories of major importance and minor importance. A nutrient a plant needs more of is called a *macronutrient,* and one it needs less of is called a *micronutrient.*

The table on the next page lists the plant nutrients, explains whether each is a macronutrient or micronutrient, and gives the source of the nutrient. It also explains which macronutrients are needed more than others. These macronutrients are labeled primary macronutrients, while those less necessary are secondary macronutrients.

The most important plant nutrients are nitrogen (N), phosphorous

Plant Nutrients

Nutrient	Type	Source
carbon (C)	macronutrient	air and water
hydrogen (H)	macronutrient	air and water
oxygen (O)	macronutrient	air and water
nitrogen (N)	macronutrient (primary)	soil and fertilizer
phosphorous (P)	macronutrient (primary)	soil and fertilizer
potassium (K)	macronutrient (primary)	soil and fertilizer
calcium (Ca)	macronutrient (secondary)	soil and fertilizer
magnesium (Mg)	macronutrient (secondary)	soil and fertilizer
sulfur (S)	macronutrient (secondary)	soil and fertilizer
iron (Fe)	micronutrient	soil and fertilizer
copper (Cu)	micronutrient	soil and fertilizer
zinc (Zn)	micronutrient	soil and fertilizer
molybdenum (Mo)	micronutrient	soil and fertilizer
boron (B)	micronutrient	soil and fertilizer
chlorine (Cl)	micronutrient	soil and fertilizer
manganese (Mn)	micronutrient	soil and fertilizer
iodine (I)	trace	soil and fertilizer
aluminum (Al)	trace	soil and fertilizer
sodium (Na)	trace	soil and fertilizer

(P), potassium (K), calcium (Ca), magnesium (Mg), and sulfur (S). Oxygen (O), carbon (C), and hydrogen (H) come from water and atmospheric carbon dioxide. Plants take in these nutrients through their roots and through the air. Micronutrients are manganese (Mg), iron (Fe), boron (B), copper (Cu), zinc (Zn), molybdenum (Mo), and chlorine (Cl). In addition, some elements, such as iodine (I) or aluminum (Al) and sodium (Na) are called trace nutrients, because they are needed in extremely minute quantities.

Positively charged nutrient ions include hydrogen (H+), calcium (Ca++), potassium (K+), magnesium (Mg++), iron (Fe++), zinc (Zn++), copper (Cu++), manganese (Mn++), and sodium (Na+) and aluminum (Al+).

Similarly charged ions repel each other. Opposite ions attract each other, as everyone knows from the cliché that opposites attract. But they have to have something to cling to in order to remain in place long enough to feel the charge from an opposite.

Here's where soil texture comes in. The smaller the soil particle the more surfaces it has, sort of like the fact that smaller people have more skin surface than bigger people. The more surfaces of negatively charged soil particles for the positively charged ions to cling to, the more nutrient-rich the soil will be.

Nitrogen is one of the most necessary nutrients of all. Unfortunately, in the form most useful to plants (nitrate, NO_3), it has a negative charge. Because soil particles are also negative, nitrates are not held in the soil and are easily leached out by rain. Additionally, decomposing organic matter uses nitrogen in the process of decomposition.

Vegetable gardeners and gardeners who love beautiful perennial gardens find themselves forced to fertilize their gardens, unless they are organic gardeners. Native plant and wildlife gardeners can take advantage of the plants' natural abilities to be healthy with whatever nutrients their native soil provides.

In addition, plant communities depend on each other, because some of the plants may well serve the others by "fixing" nitrogen, making nitrogen stick to the soil particles. In a vegetable garden, peas and beans and other legumes (in the family Leguminosae) are known for this ability. They have nodes on their roots that convert nitrites in the soil to nitrates. Some soil microbes also convert unusable forms of nitrogen to usable forms.

Soil pH and Plant Health

The pH scale is numbered from zero to fourteen, with seven as neutral (neither acid nor alkaline), and measures the hydrogen and sodium in the soil. The more sodium in the soil, the higher the pH number will be. The more hydrogen, the lower the pH number. The presence of large quantities of hydrogen (H) in the soil makes it acidic. Large amounts of sodium (Na) makes soil alkaline (or "basic" or "sweet"). This pH chart shows the range of pH tolerances for some plants. The jack-in-the-pulpit grows in boggy areas, where decaying plant matter that is wet all

pH Chart

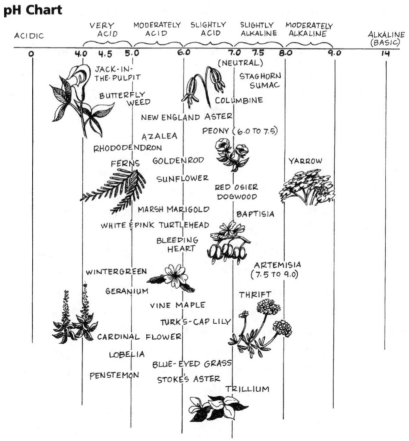

Different plants have different requirements for soil pH.

the time makes for very acidic conditions. Yarrow, on the other hand, along with artemisia, tolerate moderately alkaline conditions.

The way plant nutrients react chemically with hydrogen or sodium determines whether or not a plant can make use of them. For example, the optimum pH for microscopic soil bacteria (microbes) to change ammonium nitrogen into nitrates is between 5.5 and 7.8. These acidic soils will usually be rich in nutrients. Yet in basic soils—those with a pH greater than seven, plants have adapted to a less nutrient-rich environment.

The acidity or alkalinity of the soil determines whether plants will be happy in our gardens. For example, western Washington's soils are relatively acidic because they eroded from igneous rock, in contrast with the soils of eastern Washington, which eroded from basalt, the breakdown of ancient lava flows. Igneous rock is acidic; basalt is alkaline. The high quantity of rainfall also makes western Washington's soils relatively acidic, because the hydrogen ion is present in significant quantities in water (H_2O). In eastern Washington, with an average nine inches of annual rainfall, soils are drier and the presence of the sodium ion makes them more alkaline. Plants native to one side of the state cannot often grow successfully in gardens on the other side.

Knowing the pH of your soil will enable you to grow plants you might not otherwise think would thrive together, such as the peonies and rhododendrons, and the optimum pH encourages the zillions of soil bacteria that transform chemicals plants can't use (such as nitrites) into nutrients they can use (nitrates).

Fortunately, it's not necessary—even if we wanted to—for gardeners to become soil chemists, but the more we know about how and what plants eat, the less expensive and difficult gardening will be. For one thing, we'll have fewer problems to treat. A healthy plant throws off disease more readily and is not as stressed by attacks of predatory insects as an unhealthy plant. A healthy garden environment encourages the presence of beneficial insects, such as ladybugs, that love a diet of aphids, or beneficial nematodes that gorge themselves on root weevils.

How to Restore the Soil

When our gardens have the right soils, native plants will thrive and plant communities will foster the well-being of local wildlife. If your soil, through years of mismanagement with chemical pesticides and fertilizers, is no longer hospitable to native plants, you can bring it back. All you need is a little time and patience. You can grind up fallen leaves and put them on the ground, where they will decompose and merge into the soil. You can compost kitchen waste and dig it into the ground or spread it on top to let it become part of the soil over time. Any vegetable organic matter added to the soil will eventually become part of the healthy environment for the creatures that live in it.

We still do this, so that the garden's soil is constantly being renewed, just as in the natural cycle.

Caring for Native Plants

One of the greatest advantages of gardening with native plants is that they are adapted to the local climate. Once established, they need very little care. However, during the first weeks or the first year they're in your garden, and perhaps for longer, they may need some TLC to get going, no matter how carefully you have selected the site and prepared the soil.

In dry climates, you may need to water the plants until they are established. Watch them carefully for signs of drying out, and if they begin to show signs of wilt, add water. After the first year or two, they should be on their own.

Watering Native Plants

Native plants have adapted to the type and amount of rainfall that occurs in your region. Some wildlife gardeners choose not to supplement natural water supplies at all, and native plants can usually survive with little or no extra water on your part. But even desert plants need initial watering to establish themselves, and in periods of unusual and extended drought, you might need to think about some supplemental watering. We try to water only to lower or prevent stress on the native plants, without causing the plants to produce so much growth above ground that the roots might not be able to support it.

To water most efficiently, and with the least possible waste, two methods are available: sprinkler systems or drip irrigation. Many modern sprinkler systems have rain or moisture sensors, to optimize water use.

Another advantage of an automatic sprinkler system is that you can run it when no one else is watering and take advantage of the increased water pressure. Ours is set to go at 3:00 A.M. We run it only when plants show signs of wilting, during an unusually extended summer drought. Interestingly, we've observed that our water garden provides some atmospheric moisture by evaporation, so we need to water less even during the summer drought.

Water conservation is important throughout the West, and drip irrigation is the most efficient method of watering plants. Because it sends the water directly to the root zone, some people estimate that it saves one-third to two-thirds of the water used by an old-fashioned sprinkler. You can set up a dripline in a number of ways, either by buying drip systems or by using a standard hose and punching holes in it. Water runs out of the dripline or hose at ground level.

Two of our flower beds, devoted to attracting pollinators with flowers, lie in the driest of the garden microclimates. These beds lie under a bigleaf maple, so when the tree is leafed out, the plants below exist in a rain shadow. During August and September, when temperatures can climb into the high nineties, I attach a hose to the dripline and water late in the evening, when it's cooler. Watering then conserves water, because the sun's heat does not evaporate moisture so quickly as during the day.

Maintaining the Native Plant Garden

It's no accident that native plant garden books, even this one, discuss low maintenance rather than no maintenance.

Some wildlife gardeners neither weed nor water. Gardening with native plants means less garden maintenance, but the point of this book is making gardens, not totally reconstructing pieces of natural landscapes. And maintenance, including weeding and some watering, helps to promote the health of plant communities and the health of the wildlife that lives in them.

While some wildlife gardeners regard all plants as natives rather than weeds, I've been unable to totally wean myself from the neat-and-tidy look I was brought up with. On the neatness scale, with zero meaning totally natural (no maintenance) and ten meaning mowed and clipped (lots of maintenance), I'm probably somewhere around three. At this point, because I don't know much about native grasses, I am less tolerant of them than I might otherwise be. In the woods, hiking, I don't see grasses among the plant communities, so I don't tolerate them in the garden. I don't want them to overpower plants that are part of the community.

Every two or three years, or whenever the trees look as if they might need it, we call in the arborist to prune them. In our climate, tree pruning is best done in late January or early February, just before the sap starts to rise. I prune the shrubs—rhododendrons, spireas, viburnums, weigelas—myself. Living on the Pacific Rim, I've been influenced by the beauty of Japanese gardens. Pruning is one of the most peaceful and artistic activities in the garden, and it's necessary for the plants' health.

Having a sanctuary garden calls for a different attitude to gardening, a less controlled approach, a tolerance of untidiness and some usually less welcome beings. We don't legislate who can take sanctuary there. We feed gray squirrels, even though some people object, referring to them as fuzzy-tailed rats because they are aggressive to other squirrels and to birds and eat food intended for birds. The animals that most people consider predators or pests don't know they have a bad reputation. They are just being themselves and trying to survive. Like many of us.

Your garden will change over time. As it does, you can have the fun of adding more plants or moving some to a better location. As our garden has matured, I find I can still have the fun of introducing new plants. As I learn more, I modify the garden. The Nootka rose is a recent discovery; I'm looking forward to having roses in the garden again.

Plants tend to influence their surroundings as they grow. The bigger ones will spread out and shade the ground. If they're "happy" in a place, they will proliferate. Then you have the fun of dividing them and spreading them around the garden. One year I bought two native bleeding hearts; the next year I found two square feet of this delightful, delicate plant. Some years back, I planted hardy cyclamen, which survives in our climate nicely. Now I'm finding it all over the yard, and I'm enjoying it in surprising places, places where I didn't plant it.

When our garden becomes too crowded, we throw a "garden renovation party." We invite friends and acquaintances to come and dig out plants they want. This helps other people with their gardens and keeps ours from becoming overcrowded.

Where conditions have developed to be right for some plants, you can move them into those locations—or buy others to grow there. If over time the canopy and understory layers turn some spots from sunny to shady, you can move in shade-loving plants for the shrub and ground layers. I have gradually replaced plants as conditions changed. Where hybrid tea roses once grew, the Nootka rose flourishes. Like the other plants in the garden, it requires an acidic soil and the amount of rainfall we get. It can also handle the summer drought.

Weeds

I've often been puzzled by the term *weed*. To tidy gardeners, a weed is a plant they didn't put in. To others, it's the "wrong plant in the wrong place." In my garden, a weed isn't necessarily a weed at all; it may be a native plant and have some useful purpose in the overall ecosystem of the garden. Weeds are not pulled hastily, and sometimes not at all.

When I began gardening, I thought a weed was, as the garden books said, "the wrong plant in the wrong place." Then I realized that wasn't necessarily so, that good things could happen to the garden if I relaxed my grip and gave up some control. About the same time, I began to be more interested in the native plants of our area. As I let them into the garden, some guests were not impressed. They looked at some pretty yellow buttercups and said, "You let that grow?"

For some people, a native plant is automatically a weed. As I told one visitor, "One person's weed is another person's native plant." Since then, I've learned better. In our garden, a weed is a nonnative plant that threatens the health or life of a native plant or of the plant community, that will damage the ecosystem in the garden by running rampant and taking over or by being a menace to natural areas. Noxious weeds such as holly and herb Robert are in these categories. I also pull out flowers that have seeded themselves where we don't want them. Any perennial that tends to take over the garden is a weed. We take care to get rid of noxious weeds, those that would cause problems in natural areas (see chapter 6, "Benign Pest Control"), and anything in the pathways and the patios is a weed. So, we pull it. Weeds should also be controlled to protect native plant populations from invasion and possible displacement.

In my case, redefining the term *weed* took time. But gardeners can develop an appreciation for native plants, so instead of thinking of them as weeds, we can see their beauty. I used to pull out fireweed. But seeing stands of it in open areas has persuaded me that despite its name, it is a pretty pink flower that makes a flamboyant show in the summertime (see Plate 7, following page 68). The plants also have beautiful seed heads in fall. Bees love them, too.

We clean up the areas immediately around the house to prevent fires during the summer drought, when things dry out. We are careful not to leave piles of brush or dead wood; we mulch what we can and add it to the compost piles. Otherwise, we call in people who specialize in removing brush and dead limbs from trees.

Native Plant Controversies

Like most concepts people grasp hold of, gardening with native plants has its controversial aspects. One approach demands that we plant only individual native plants that may have existed in the immediate vicinity. Another demands that gardeners reproduce exactly the plant communities that once existed there. A third approach holds that reproducing the original ecosystem is impossible because urban areas have changed the climate in which the plants once existed.

Some claim that indigenous wildlife, such as hummingbirds, will only recognize native plants as food. But thousands of gardeners, myself included, have watched hummers busily feeding from plastic feeders, as well as nonnative species of coral bells (*Heuchera* species), various columbines, and other plants introduced for the hummingbirds' benefit.

Certainly the great blue heron did not fail to recognize the koi in our water garden a few years ago; it knew a fish when it saw one. Having eaten them, it moved on. A species of native bee that nests underground is very busy among all the flowers in the garden, including the Japanese anemones.

While some people insist that a sanctuary garden is an exact re-creation of the natural landscape, it is not necessary to exactly recreate the natural landscape in order to give sanctuary to wildlife. To qualify for the Washington State designation, we provided an inventory of native plants on the lot, but as you know by now, we also grow some exotics—the oft-mentioned peonies, nonnative rhododendrons, Japanese anemones, foxglove, columbine, hardy cyclamen, various flowering shrubs, and ajuga.

Your sanctuary garden can incorporate a mix of native plants with your own favorite exotics, with one caveat. If part of your aim in making a wildlife sanctuary garden is to help save the planet one yard at a time, you owe it to the surrounding environment not to plant anything identified as a noxious weed. A noxious weed is a plant that will run rampant throughout the natural areas and drive out the native plants. Just a short time ago, I checked the Washington State University Extension Web site for *stewardship gardening* and discovered that herb Robert is now classed as a noxious weed. I've been making war on it ever since. We have a lovely native bleeding heart, *Dicentra formosa,* with finely incised leaves and delicate pink flowers that droop like the other bleeding hearts. It grows only a few inches tall, in shady, wooded areas with acidic soil. Herb Robert, which grows about the same height and also has incised leaves and pink flowers, could rapidly overpower the bleeding heart. For years, debate raged over purple loosestrife, with some botanists claiming that one cultivar was sterile. When at last scientists discovered that the sterile cultivar, or cultivated variety, was capable of reproducing when crossed with the nonsterile cultivar, purple loosestrife, too, joined the noxious weed list.

For the most current list, consult your local botanical garden or extension office. Both may well have a Web site to make your research easier. The Ohio State University Extension even maintains an extensive online bibliography of plants native to the regions of Ohio.

Putting It All Together

Any plant will make its contribution to your garden. But it's you, the gardener, who will decide what contribution you want made, and what contribution you want to make through this garden of yours. This chapter has provided you with some recommendations, suggestions, and guidelines. Now it's up to you. Have fun.

Chapter 4

Attracting Animals

On a cold, drizzly November day when the clouds have settled down low enough to touch and all I want to do is stay inside where it's warm and dry, the garden is bright and cheerful and alive with motion and color amid the gray drizzle and the soft greens of rainy leaves. The birds are competing at the feeders and in the berry shrubs. Blue Steller's jays jeer at the weather; yellow evening grosbeaks imitate sunshine; and flashes of red herald the northern flicker and red-winged blackbird. Squirrels chase each other around tree trunks and perform their trapeze acts among the branches. The weather outside may be damp and dreary, but joy lightens my soul from watching so much activity and from knowing that we are contributing to these creatures' survival. The photo opposite shows a native Douglas squirrel from Carol Siipola's garden feeding on peanuts with typical squirrel agility. These antics are guaranteed to brighten the dullest spirits.

Liveliness and cheer are a good portion of the blessing in sanctuary gardening. The show changes with the seasons and as animals come and go. Migrant birds pass through for a bite and a rest along their journey. Red-winged blackbirds drop by for a visit on their forays out from their nesting sites in a neighboring wetland. Come spring, a mallard pair

This native Douglas squirrel is concentrating on his dinner, not his circus act.

lands for a swim and a snack on snails' eggs or emerging plants in the water garden.

Some birds have taken up residence here. The sparrows are always around, as are the house finches. The northern flickers are constantly feeding at the suet, and the ringneck doves are occasional visitors from their nesting sites in the nearby greenbelt. We have our favorites, of course, the flickers and the white ringneck doves, but everyone is welcome, even when they cause some damage.

At night, when the birds are tucked up resting, the nocturnal animals come out. Possums and raccoons visit in the dark, but we occasionally see them in the winter when we get up in the dark to go to work.

Sometimes we only know some animals have been here because of the traces they leave. Fish scales on the path by the pond and overturned water-lily pots were probably the work of a raccoon. That ended my second (and last) attempt to keep koi. The great blue heron ended the first attempt.

I learned a valuable lesson from my attempts to keep koi. I had traded water plants for koi at a water garden nursery, because I was intrigued by these beautiful fish, members of the carp family. I named a white one that I enjoyed seeing every day in the pond Moby Koi. Then one day, I couldn't find it. When I found scales on the path, I mourned a little. Then an orange, white, and black koi disappeared, and I knew something was after them. But who? One by one, they all disappeared.

Early one Sunday morning a neighbor knocked at our door. He'd seen a great blue heron on our chimney. Then we knew. That bird had eaten them. I began to find ways of excluding herons from the garden. Someone suggested a heron look-alike statue, so I put one up. For a while, we had no more visitations from heron. I tried black koi, thinking they'd be invisible.

They, too, disappeared, and the water-lily pots were overturned. This had to be raccoons. I sought ways of keeping raccoons out of the garden, but some of the methods seemed ludicrous. Bottled fox urine? That might work, but it would drive the dogs nuts.

We talked it over and decided on a policy that rules this garden to this day. While we were disappointed because we liked the koi, we reasoned that the raccoons and the herons weren't deliberately committing crimes. They were just being what they were, animals crowded out of their habitats by urban sprawl and desperate to survive. We couldn't exclude any wild creature.

I took down the heron look-alike. A few months later, when I went into the kitchen, I saw a live heron standing in the pond. I was awestruck. This great smoky-blue bird, like a work of art, a sculpture, had struck his still pose in the lower pond. I was privileged to watch until, with a sudden flap of his enormous wings, he took off. He was being a heron, doing what herons do—fishing for his dinner. With the decimation of wetlands in western Washington, he had to look somewhere, and flying overhead he had found our pond again.

Making a backyard wildlife sanctuary garden, inviting nature in, to us, means we welcome all creatures, including the ugly and the creepy crawlies, the beautiful, the comical, and the cute. We don't exclude an animal from the sanctuary because we don't like it or we're afraid of it or it has some loathsome quality such as its smell or its feeding habits (see chapter 6, on pests, for ways of dealing with the truly obnoxious or harmful wild animals).

Humans make too many value judgments about the animals in our gardens. I've heard people say that starlings are too aggressive and rob native species of birds of food. Of course, everyone hates or fears snakes. At least many people do. Myself, I don't mind them. I feel differently about poisonous snakes, but the coiled garden snake in Plate 8 (following page 116) won't harm a human. Snakes kill mice, who must also have some part in the scheme of things. While starlings are one of three wild bird species (along with pigeons and house sparrows) unprotected by federal law, their aggression might be to a robin's advantage. I've seen starlings flocking together with red-winged blackbirds in winter. Maybe they're intruders into those flocks, but maybe not.

We've worked to make an ecosystem with plant communities, but the animals are part of that ecosystem, too. Until we know that a particular creature is destroying the ecosystem, we won't move to prevent its residence, either full- or part-time. With animals coming in from outside, as the heron did, the wildlife garden becomes part of the greater ecosystem.

Dealing with Big Wildlife

Some wildlife may be a bit much to handle. When a large or potentially dangerous animal comes into your yard, there are several things you can do. First, be cautious but tolerate the big wild creatures if they come around. If you're frightened, or if the animal—a cougar or a bear—might be dangerous in urban and suburban areas, call your local animal control office.

Second, keep your pets indoors.

Third, never get between a mother and her young. Even human mothers can be fiercely protective of their babies, and animal mothers will quickly go on the offensive if they perceive a threat to their offspring.

Usually, in urban or suburban areas, wild animals move into yards because they are being crowded out of their own areas. One man said, "It's not so much they who are in our backyard, it's us who are in their front yards." Another cause of wild animals in the yard is our own sentimentality. We just can't kill Bambi or Thumper, so they overpopulate areas to their own and others' detriment. Overpopulated deer starve because they are not hunted and because their natural predators have been decimated. The result is herds of deer in the gardens and villages with more deer than people. The natural ecosystem has broken down.

Some wildlife can be downright dangerous. I recently asked people in the Internet Wildlife Garden Forum what they do about big wildlife. The responses surprised me. Not one person actively sought to destroy the big intruders, which ranged from cougars to moose and grizzly bears (in Alaska). All of the notes displayed a wide tolerance for and love of wildlife in all of its forms.

Barb in Michigan wrote:

> We had mountain lions on our property occasionally when I lived in Texas. They travel a circuit of about 100 miles in their search for food. Our main reaction was not to tell anyone about them, since they would probably be killed. The big wild animals are usually not dangerous to people, with a few exceptions: if you get between them and their young, if the animal has been injured, often by being shot by a poorly trained hunter, if the animal is very old and cannot hunt as well as it did in its prime, if people feed them so they lose their fear of humans, or if the animal was raised by humans and then returned to the wild. Most big game will run the other way as fast as you do.

Regarding alligators, Caitlin wrote:

In Florida, it is not unusual to see alligators on the golf courses. They are basically left alone, too. There are occasional reports of disappearing dogs and other pets, but what do you expect from an alligator, anyway?!

Joannie, who lives in the Sierra Nevada, wrote her recommendations for dealing with cougars:

We have a mountain lion behind our house. We have found his footprints about ten feet from our bedroom window. The only real problem with the cat is that it is a male and has marked his territory. The smell is quite strong! It makes tomcat urine smell like the finest perfume! My little dog won't even walk in that direction anymore. The mountain lions have eaten a couple of dogs around here in the past, but only when they are tied up and too easy to get. We live in the Sierra Nevadas and are used to big animals hanging around.

So is Susan in Alaska. She wrote about her experiences with bears and moose. Moose, she reports, can range in size from 900 to 1,500 lbs. While she understands some people's fear of big wild animals and doesn't "want to come nose-to-nose with a bear in the woods" herself, she reports, "These encounters are ones of mutual curiosity and harmony."

So it was startling at first when she looked a moose in the face:

In one of those incongruous moments when things don't go as usual, a young moose living near our house came up onto our porch and looked in the living room at us. He was so curious! He walked around the house and looked in every window, including the bathroom. We followed him and I touched our side of the window while his nose was against the other side. Big close-up of moose face! My daughter was in the bathroom and looked up to see this huge, hairy face staring in at her.

On a silent winter night brilliant with stars, Susan and her husband returned home from a party:

> *As we walked from our car to our back door, along the narrow path beside our house, I was thinking how heart-shattering beautiful it is where I live, when my husband, moving several feet ahead of me, quietly said, "Moose." I looked up and in the quiet night we were walking in front of a moose who stood about ten feet away, facing us. He was calmly munching on willows in our yard, a dark shadow of a moose in the starlit night. It was one of the more magical moments of my life. I love the big animals!*

Meeting up with a moose is one thing, because these animals are not usually dangerous. But bears? To suburbanites in the Lower Forty-eight, the thought of meeting a bear can be frightening. However, Susan reports:

> *I love big wildlife in the garden. Black bears aren't so very big. But nothing, and I mean NOTHING prepared me for the awe-inspiring sight of my first grizzly. It was the most fantastic, frightening, thrilling thing I've ever seen in my life. No photo, no words, not even a movie on the big screen can impart what it is like to see a grizzly in action in the wild. It is stunning!*
>
> *Before we got siding up on our house, while we were building it, one night I was alone and a bear was clawing at the tar paper that was all that separated me from it. I was nervous, yes, but I'm still here to tell the tale. I wouldn't get rid of the bears because of it. I might, however, run for the camera and the bear mace at the same time, just in case.*

She concludes:

> *My greatest sorrow in life is that humans do not value the animals and the rest of nature enough to ensure that we have nature with us always, that we value commerce and lack of controls on ourselves and material wealth more.*

As urban sprawl decimates habitats, more suburbanites in the Lower Forty-eight may at some point encounter wildlife. Sometimes, as with deer and Canada geese overrunning towns and metropolitan areas, solutions are difficult. When the larger predatory animals come into suburban or urban areas, the best thing people can do is to leave them alone.

As these animals lose their fear of humans, we will inevitably encounter them more often. By following these simple rules, suburbanites may spare themselves some grief:

1. Never attempt to feed them by hand or leave pet food outside where a wild animal can get it. Feed dogs and cats and other pets indoors.

2. Do not attempt to make a pet of a wild animal. Some animals become fixated on human beings or lose their fear of people. In either case, when they outgrow the cute stage, they will not be able to survive in the wild.

3. If a bear, cougar, or coyote is reported in your area, bring your pets inside. A dog tied up in the backyard may become an easy target for a wild animal. This is not a quick, clean death; wild predators bring down their prey and tear them apart, eating their prey while it is still alive.

4. Do not, under any circumstances, attempt to approach or interfere with a wild animal. Call your local animal control office.

5. If you find a baby wild animal, it is probably not lost. The mother has probably left it there while she forages for food. Never come between a mother bear and her young. Nothing can be so fierce as a mother's—human or animal—protective instinct for her young.

6. If necessary, call the county animal control office to remove the animal. Animal control officers, who are trained in wildlife removal, will do it humanely with a tranquilizer and relocate the

animal further away. Relocation, of course, is not always the best solution, because the animal will have to compete for food and mates with the current inhabitants. But for the occasional cougar that stakes out an urban neighborhood as its territory, relocation is the best solution.

Import Wildlife?

Attracting wildlife is really rather simple. If you provide the right food, water, and shelter in a habitat to their liking, the wild creatures will come. You will not have to import them. As a matter of fact, wildlife gardening experts, such as Flora Skelly of Seattle, are adamant that wildlife should never be brought into a wildlife garden. "The habitat may not have just what the animal needs," says Skelly, "and you could be doing more harm than good."

Attracting Birds

Bringing birds into the garden is almost breathtakingly simple. Start with a feeder or three and year-round water. Buy the food at a recognized store that caters to wild creatures, if you can, rather than at a pet food store.

When to Feed Birds

We feed birds year-round. At first, we fed them only in the winter. While plenty of habitat remained around us, we were not worried that birds would starve in the summer. But after the last thirteen acres of natural area were turned into a housing development in 1994, we decided to try to take up some of the slack.

Some people recommend stopping the feeding in summer so that birds will not become dependent on food you provide. If you've heard that you should stop feeding birds in the summer for this reason, take heart. You don't have to forego the fun of attracting birds merely because food plants have come into fruit. The food you supply in summer is merely a supplement to the natural foods they find. Seed-eating birds

This northern flicker is oblivious to winter's rain because he is getting enough suet to eat.

have a tough time in summer, when the previous season's natural supply is gone and this year's seeds have not yet formed. We set out suet, too, until the weather warms up enough to spoil it, but a friend of ours hangs suet even on the hottest days because, even if it melts, he says, the birds will still eat. Our suet feeders are in the shade, and the flickers are constant visitors to them, as they are to the suet feeder shown above. On a wet winter day, this northern flicker is feasting on a suet cake, while a pileated woodpecker watches for an opportunity.

How to Feed Birds

Besides water, birds need two components in their diet in order to be healthy: the proper food for their species and grit. Birds don't have teeth. They have a crop, or gizzard, in which they collect tiny pieces of sand, rock, or eggshells. Our paths and patios are made of a type of crushed rock, so birds can find all the grit they need. In winter, if snow covers these places, we shovel it away so the birds can reach the grit.

Birds find grit in the streets, too. Many cities use a type of rock salt to keep the streets clear. Homeowners also sometimes resort to this quick method of clearing snow from driveways. Salt will kill birds or make them sick. If you're concerned that birds might accidentally ingest salt from the street or from your walkways, you can set out a platform feeder with crushed eggshells or sand. As long as you keep the feeder free of snow and constantly supplied, the birds will be satisfied.

To save yourself trouble and inconvenience during inclement weather, place the feeders where it's most convenient and where you can see them from inside the house. We have feeders in the backyard and in the front, so we can have the fun of seeing the activity from the kitchen and from the living room (see Plate 9, following page 116).

If your wildlife gardening is primarily to attract birds, place the feeders where squirrels can't get into them easily. The experts at the Audubon Society and the U.S. Fish and Wildlife Service (FWS) recommend a clear space of at least ten feet around each feeder. This distance helps to prevent squirrels from jumping onto the feeder. Having shrubs or trees at that distance gives small birds shelter from predators. When they spot danger, they can quickly fly to a neighboring shrub and disappear into it. When we open the front door, the birds fly into the laurels. If we hadn't seen them hide, we wouldn't know there were any birds around.

We've placed the feeders where they are easy for us to get to, but our climate (USDA zone eight) is relatively mild. The coldest winters we have may produce snow a foot or so deep for a few days, but in parts of the country, in the Northern Tier states of Montana, North Dakota, Minnesota, or Maine, where winters are fiercely cold and long, you may have to think about putting the feeders where you can get to them through the drifts. If you have a sheltered place out of the wind, so much the better for both you and the birds.

In places with hard winters, the water in your birdbaths will freeze solid. You might investigate a small warmer for melting ice in birdbaths or a larger one for ponds. Some conscientious wildlife gardeners care so much about their wildlife gardens that they aren't content to break the ice twice a day, in the morning and in the evening; they drive home from work at lunchtime to break it, too.

With the growing popularity of bird-watching and feeding, the manufacture of bird feeders has become a significant industry. Bird feeders, it seems, now come in every style imaginable.

According to the FWS, there are six main points to consider when buying a bird feeder:

- How durable is it?
- Will it keep the seeds dry?
- How easy is it to clean?
- How much seed will it hold?
- How many birds will it feed at one time?
- Which species will use it?

How long a feeder will last depends on the material it's made of, the weather, and how often you clean it. Feeders need cleaning periodically to get rid of bird droppings and old seed, particularly if the seed is wet. While plastic is easy to clean, squirrels' sharp teeth can chew through it, and you may have to buy a new feeder sooner than you would like. Some types of wood are better than others for outdoor use. In desert areas, you may need to consider wood that resists drying out, perhaps manzanita, while in damp climates such woods as plantation teak or western red cedar may be a good solution. Be sure to ask if the wood comes from trees that are becoming scarce. You will be doing a favor for wildlife in other parts of the globe. Using teak grown on plantations does not endanger the ecosystems of natural areas where teak grows.

Keeping the seeds dry is important, because damp seeds rot, and rotting seeds breed fungi that can kill birds. Even feeders made of materials impervious to rain, such as plastic or wood, will let rainwater in through the feeding holes. Platform feeders, even those with drainage holes, may collect water and brew an unhealthy soup if they're not cleaned out whenever necessary. Our platform feeder seems to work well, although it has no drainage holes, because it has a roof. Seed does not last long in it, but I take a stick or a miniature shovel for indoor plants and clean it out when I suspect it needs it, sometimes two or three times a week during the ten-month rainy season.

You can clean glass or plastic feeders periodically with hot water and soap, as you would wash dishes, but with a little bleach added to fight stubborn bacteria. Just be sure to have the bleach well rinsed out so it does not poison the animals. Wood feeders may be cleaned the same way. Bleach might fade the wood, but wood fades over time anyhow. Hummingbird feeders need cleaning often, perhaps two or three times a week, to prevent the nectar from fermenting.

How big the feeder should be depends on how much you want to spend on seed and what species of birds you want to attract. A feeder large enough to accommodate the bigger birds—jays and flickers, for example—also provides room for squirrels to sit and dine at their leisure if the feeder is too close to shrubs. The photo below shows several types of feeders at the condominium home of our friends Roxie and Denis, in the Puget Sound region. With a master's degree in wildlife ecology, emphasizing wild birds, Denis has designed the feeder stations for maximum benefit to the birds in their area.

A hummingbird feeder should be considerably smaller than feeders for other birds. According to the FWS, a hummingbird will drink less than an ounce a day, and it's a territorial bird. Once a hummer stakes out

These birds enjoy their dinners at an arrangement of feeders on a condominium patio.

its territory, it will not share with another hummingbird. That goes for feeders, too. Hummingbirds, it seems, are not as sociable as chickadees and house finches; they do not congregate at a feeder, so a large feeder can be wasteful.

Instead of using feeders for hummingbirds, we have three varieties of honeysuckle (including two native species) to attract them. I've also seen them darting among the coral bells and the foxglove, and sipping at the water in our ponds.

Ultimately, how large a feeder you need and how many you use depend on your situation. If you live where animals spend the winter, you may need more feeders. On the other hand, you may wish to limit the number of birds by putting up smaller feeders or feeding only certain species.

What to Feed Birds

Different species of birds have different requirements for a balanced diet. The FWS reports that goldfinches, chickadees, and woodpeckers like black oil sunflower and feed from a tubular feeder. We have also observed house finches and sparrows at our tubular feeder.

Different types of birds prefer different feeds, in different feeders. For example, house sparrows, juncos, towhees, and doves prefer a platform feeder with millet. Nectar is not only the food of the gods, but of hummingbirds and woodpeckers, orioles, and cardinals. Fruit eaters include orioles, mockingbirds, woodpeckers, and cedar waxwings. Woodpeckers also love hanging suet feeders; we've seen red-crested and pileated woodpeckers and northern flickers at our suet feeders. Some birds, such as woodpeckers and chickadees, can eat peanuts, and jays, juncos, starlings, and woodpeckers also eat peanut butter suet. Some birds like peanuts, but don't give them peanuts that are preroasted for humans. You may enjoy commercial peanuts, but they will kill the birds.

The following table offers some recommendations for which types of food are preferred by some of the more common types of birds. Not every bird is listed, however. Ask your local Audubon Society to determine the best foods for your local bird populations. The URL for the national Audubon Society's Web site is www.audubon.org.

What to Feed Birds

To Attract This Bird	Use This Food
American goldfinch	millet, black oil sunflower seeds, hulled sunflower seeds, niger thistle
American robin	berries, fruit, occasional seeds
bluebird	peanut butter suet, fruit
blue jay	peanut kernel, acorns, black oil sunflower, corn, fruit
bobwhite quail	corn
bushtit	suet
California quail	millet, milo, fine cracked corn
cardinal (G)	black oil sunflower, peanut butter suet, fruit, peanuts, nectar
chickadee	black oil sunflower seeds, peanuts, suet, niger thistle
crossbill (G)	black oil sunflower seeds
dark-eyed junco	millet, peanut butter suet, corn, peanuts, niger thistle
duck (mallard)	aquatic grasses, other water plants
duck (wood)	acorns, beech nuts, aquatic grasses, other water plants
evening grosbeak	black oil sunflower, black-striped sunflower seeds
flicker	suet
gray catbird	raisins
house finch	millet, black oil sunflower, peanuts, niger thistle, nectar
house sparrow (G)	millet, hulled sunflower, canary seed, fine cracked corn, peanuts
hummingbird	sugar-water (nectar)
mourning dove	millet, black oil sunflower seeds, fine cracked corn, peanuts, niger thistle
nuthatch	suet, black oil sunflower seeds
oriole	nectar
pine siskin	millet, black oil sunflower seeds, niger thistle
purple finch	black oil sunflower seeds, niger thistle, nectar
rock dove	millet, milo, fine cracked corn
rufous-sided towhee	millet
song sparrow	millet
starling	milo, peanut heart, oats, suet, corn, peanuts, fruit
thrush	nectar, fruit
white-crowned sparrow	millet, black oil sunflower seeds
wren	suet
woodpecker	suet, peanut suet, black oil sunflower seeds, fruit, nectar

(G) = ground feeder. Feed ground-feeding birds on platforms or trays.
This table is compiled from several sources, primarily *Gardening for Wildlife*, the Washington State Department of Fish and Wildlife, and the FWS Web site (URL: www.fws.gov/r9mbmo/pamphlet/attract.htm).

Plate 4. This plant community composed of exotic heathers and rhododendrons mixes well with the native ferns and western red huckleberry.

Plate 5. The bees love to feast on asters in late summer and early autumn.

Plate 6. This snag functions as a food source for birds and as a garden accent.

Plate 7. The lowly native fireweed can be a spectacular perennial, if we know how to see it. It's not a weed.

The more different types of feeders you use the more species of birds you will attract. The different styles ensure that birds get food in ways that are most compatible with their habits. We use ground feeders for birds that eat on the ground. These are easy to make. Simply take a piece of scrap wood, drill holes for drainage, and set it on something that raises it a few inches off the ground. Plate 10 (following page 116) shows a group of native doves congregated at a feeder in the Puget Sound region. A piece of plywood is placed on the ground with seed piled on it. When we were there, we waited quietly for about half an hour, until the birds thought we were part of the landscape, and then they came to pose.

We have a burning pit ringed with cement blocks that is unused now that our county has prohibited outside burning. The ground feeder is about two inches off the ground and drains into the pit.

A platform feeder invites larger birds, such as jays or ringneck doves, or flocks of small ones. As many as a dozen sparrows or finches will use the feeder at one time, but not without squabbling. Another feeder is a clear plastic tubular feeder on a pole that we use for black sunflower seeds. For suet, you can use a house-type feeder with suet holders at both ends or suet hangers, which are open wire boxes. We hang those from tree branches.

As a wildlife gardener, you may find the major food sources in your yard come from the plants you use in your landscaping. We have three species of wild berries: salmonberry, thimbleberry, and huckleberry. All of the plants were either here originally or have been introduced— usually by birds, we suspect. In addition, we have planted other fruiting shrubs such as pyracantha and dogwood shrubs.

When we first moved into the house seventeen years ago, we put in a sour cherry tree that birds have regularly stripped each summer before we or the neighbors can pick the cherries for pies. Recently the sour cherry has been added to the list of possibly noxious weeds for western Washington, because the birds who plant thimbleberries in our yard may also plant sour cherry trees in the natural areas. Sharing the cherries with the neighbors makes friends for the sanctuary, which is quite different from the lawns surrounding us. So far, we have no plans to cut it down, but we have encouraged the neighbors to pick the cherries before the birds can get them. Another solution would be to put a net over the tree to prevent birds from eating the cherries.

The dwarf three-way apple tree, on the other hand, gives wild areas no problems; it contributes its fruit to the wild creatures until they have eaten all the apples. We and the neighbors take what apples we can use and leave the rest on the tree. Little by little, they are eaten.

All year long, there are several sources of native foods for birds. The cascara trees have small black berries in July, followed by seeds in the winter. The small local variety of Oregon grape (*Mahonia nervosa*) has lovely yellow flowers in the spring, followed by berries in late June. The white flowers of the native red osier dogwood yield to berries in August.

Compatible exotic plants also help to feed the birds. The pyracantha, a thorny shrub, has red berries in winter.

Besides berry plants, the birds can always dine on the caterpillars and other larvae that would munch up the plants. Because we don't use chemicals to repel insects from the plants, birds can always find something tasty to eat.

Cleanup

As any pet owner knows, cleanup is part of keeping animals, whether you have to change a cat box or follow your dog on walks with a plastic bag. To avoid bird droppings where you don't want them, particularly if you have toddlers, keep the feeders far enough away from the house or patio areas so your small children don't find them, yet close enough for you to enjoy the birds' activities. To prevent bird droppings from fouling places where children play, keep feeders away from these areas.

Cleanliness around the bird feeder is also a factor in where you place the feeders. If you decide to use a windowbox feeder, be prepared to clean the window or the house siding more frequently. For the birds' sake, scoop up leftover seed and black oil sunflower shells from the ground around the feeder and get rid of them, either in a part of your garden where they can safely decompose, or in the garbage, depending on local environmental laws. Some birds will feed on the ground, on the seed dropped from the feeder. Droppings mixed into this food can be lethal to them.

If you feed unhulled sunflower seeds, the cracked hulls will build up under your feeder, as deep as you allow. You can leave hulls under the feeder to provide a clear space, or put them in your compost pile or yard waste recycling bin, if your area has such a program. Alternatively, you might spread them around to prevent weeds in other parts of the garden.

Attracting Frogs and Other Amphibians

While feeding birds is popular, attracting other types of wildlife to a garden is often overlooked. In some people's minds, frogs aren't beautiful, or even especially cute or entertaining. They are shy creatures; sometimes I only know they are around by the sound of their croaking and the splash as they dive into the ponds.

If your locale already has frogs and amphibians, you can make an environment suitable for them, and they will find it, if a safe route exists from their original habitat, such as a nearby bog or marsh. Under no circumstance should you ever import frogs or other amphibians. If they don't come on their own, the environment is not suitable for them. They are the best judges of where they will thrive—or even survive.

Attracting frogs and protecting them can be important to an area's ecology, however, because they are a necessary part of the scheme of things. In a natural wetland, frogs eat insects, some fish fry, and snail larvae. Their greatest usefulness to humanity may be to eat many times their weight in mosquitoes. In our ponds, they form part of the cleanup crew, and without them the water garden's underwater ecosystem would not have the healthy balance necessary to support life.

Frogs (and toads) aren't the only amphibians that need a haven, though. Amphibians of all sorts are welcome to our water garden. Each has its place here. Salamanders contribute their bits as a vital link in the garden's ecosystem—and they're fun to watch.

If you put in a habitat water garden, enjoy the clutter of plants around it. In any part of the garden, being too tidy discourages amphibians. Be aware that any chemicals you use close to the wet areas could leak into them and kill or maim frogs, whose skins are extremely sensitive to toxins.

Everything you do to enrich the soil helps amphibians. For example, if you allow autumn's fallen leaves to remain on the ground and decompose naturally, frogs (and other small creatures) will hibernate under them. The winter's rains decompose the leaves and make a wet place for frogs to hibernate in. Or you could grind the leaves up and spread the fine mulch around during the winter. After raking leaves off the gravel pathways and patios in the fall, I sometimes leave a pile of leaves in the yard over winter. In the mid- or late spring, I spread the leaves out, gingerly, so as not to disturb creatures before they're ready to migrate back to the wetland habitat.

Flora Skelly has suggestions for attracting amphibians and for making habitats for amphibians, many of which arise naturally when gardening for wildlife. Amphibians need plenty of shelter from predators and toxins in their environment, so Skelly recommends that we make or keep hiding places: piles of rocks or broken concrete, logs, old firewood, stumps, root wads, and other woody debris, especially in wet areas.

Skelly also recommends that we protect any small-mammal burrows next to ponds and other water sources. Some amphibians will occupy these dens when the original inhabitants have abandoned them.

Not all frogs live year-round in the water. Many species will migrate between a pond or bog and drier parts of your garden. Skelly reminds us to "protect known migration paths from automobiles and lawn mowers." In fact, if we have some lawn, she recommends that we leave some of it unmowed, especially adjacent to those parts of the garden that are designed as wildlife habitat areas. If we do mow, she would like to see us herd any amphibians to a safe place first.

It's important not to introduce species of amphibians from other parts of the country. Water garden mail-order houses offer bullfrog tadpoles, but Skelly points out that bullfrogs are carnivorous to smaller, local species of frogs.

An invitation to a frog doesn't have to be large or elaborate. All you need is a shallow hole lined with plastic and filled with water. If you wish, you can make it into a bog garden.

To make a bog garden, first dig a shallow hole. Some experts recommend a few inches to less than a foot deep, but if you dig your hole deep enough for bog plants and add enough dirt for them, it will be a usable depth. Taper the sides gradually, at about a forty-five-degree angle, so from the side, the hole would look like a dinner plate or a wide soup bowl. This makes it easier for creatures to climb in and out.

Second, line the hole with plastic to prevent the water from seeping or draining out. You can use special water garden liners or heavy builder's plastic.

Then put dirt in the hole up to the depth the plants like. Covering the plastic with soil and leaves will prolong the life of the plastic, because the sun's UV rays cause plastic to break down over time. Line the sides with small rocks, so any small mammal that falls in can climb out again.

Next, plant native bog plants or compatible exotics that like to have their roots in water all the time. Louisiana irises do well in our upper pond, which has become more of a bog in the past few years as dirt from the banks has eroded into it. Avoid any plants that could escape and become noxious weeds in the natural areas. Other plants might include arrowhead, pickerelweed, cattails, and sedges.

Frogs are cold-blooded creatures. They take their body temperature from the air around them. They need both places to bask in the sun and places for shade when the weather is too hot. A rock or small floating log in the middle of the pond would allow them to climb out to get warm, but they would be able to dive into the water for safety. Around the perimeter, plant sheltering shrubs and plants that overhang the water. You need not fuss about tidying the edges of the bog garden. Let dead leaves remain in the water to become part of the natural bottom.

If frogs find the environment to their liking, they will come. If you don't get frogs, it may be because something about the environment is not to their liking. Think about it. Do some research at your library or by getting in touch with the local wildlife agency, extension service, the FWS, or a biologist at a local college. Or do a search on the Internet for the words *amphibian habitat, frog habitat, wild garden,* or similar phrases. If you enter the word *frog,* you will get thousands of pages, many of which may have nothing to do with the amphibian critters.

Attracting Bats

For centuries, people have feared bats, and their fear of the vampire bat in particular found expression in the Dracula legend. Vampire bats, however, do not live in North America. Even in Europe, they are more interested in cows and chickens. Because bats have been thought to be carriers of rabies, they have been exterminated in vast numbers, and their populations have been decimated because of widespread use of pesticides and destruction of their habitats.

Bats actually present little or no hazard to humans. In the wild, bat droppings decompose quickly, and bats are unlikely to prey on humans, since we aren't their natural food. They're not interested in human hair, as some fearful myths would have us believe. In fact, they will do their best to avoid us, and they're nearly always successful. Bats navigate by echolocation, a method similar to sonar; they make a clicking sound that bounces off nearby surfaces and warns them of imminent collisions. Because of this navigation system, bats are unlikely to bump into us.

The value of bats to humanity is only now being revealed to the public. Bats eat vast quantities of insects; when bats come out to feed at dusk, they eat the flying insects that make our lives miserable: gypsy moths, Japanese beetles, flying ants, crane flies, midges, and mosquitoes. It is estimated that one bat can eat 600 mosquitoes in an hour.

According to the National Wildlife Federation, bats are found in all the states, but the most common are the red bat, which eats beetles, and the big brown bat and the little brown bat, which like houses and barns to roost in. The Mexican free-tailed bat is found in drier parts of the West and Southwest and is the bat that lives in New Mexico's Carlsbad Caverns.

Bats roost in hollows in snags, in natural hollows in rocks, and in caves. In Austin, Texas, they roost by the thousands under bridges, from which they emerge at dusk to help rid the city of insects. They hibernate in the winter and are active in warmer months.

To encourage bats to come to your garden, attract insects by planting as wide a range of native flowers and shrubs as you have room for. When they have a good food source, bats will accept your invitation to come for supper. If you're concerned about mosquitoes breeding in your pond or bog garden, bats can help to take care of any potential mosquito problem. The presence of water will attract bats looking for a drink and a source of food.

But you can do something to encourage them. You can build a bat house. It should be near your pond or bog garden, between ten and fifteen feet off the ground, made of rough, untreated lumber, and attached to a permanent structure such as a pole or your house. Place it so the animal is sheltered from extreme heat and cold.

If you want plans for building a bat house or if you want more information about bats in general, contact Bat Conservation International, P.O. Box 162603, Austin, TX 78716. Or consult the *National Wildlife Federation's Guide to Gardening for Wildlife* by Craig Tufts and Peter Loewer.

Attracting Butterflies

Along with hummingbirds and bees, butterflies are important to agriculture and to gardeners as pollinators. In their search for nectar to eat, butterflies carry pollen from flower to flower, fertilizing the female parts of plants with the male pollen. From the fertilized flowers come seeds and fruits. Because different kinds of butterflies prefer or can live on only certain plants, they carry the pollen of one black-eyed Susan, for example, to another.

Only a few of the roughly 700 species of butterfly in North America are agricultural pests in their larval, or caterpillar, stage. Fruit trees such as cherry, apple, and plum can host many butterfly caterpillars, among them spring azure and viceroy. The giant swallowtail caterpillar feeds on orange trees. The caterpillar of the nonnative cabbage white, which was introduced into this continent in the mid-nineteenth century, eats cabbages, cauliflower, and other vegetables such as radishes, as well as flowers such as nasturtiums. Both are subject to heavy spraying, particularly in agricultural areas.

If you're concerned about butterfly caterpillars eating your plants, you can depend on the other life in the garden to control caterpillars, if you are not using insecticides. (See chapter 6, "Benign Pest Control," for information on controlling garden pests naturally.) Caterpillars have many enemies—birds, other insects, and spiders.

But if giant swallowtail and cabbage white butterfly larvae are pests, the harvester butterfly is one of a gardener's best friends. Both the larva and the adult feed on aphids. So far as I know, the harvester is the only carnivorous butterfly on this continent. Gardeners east of the Mississippi should gladly welcome this creature, and we Westerners should be a little envious! The harvester is found east of the Mississippi and into central Texas in the South.

Another caterpillar, the larva of the great purple hairstreak, eats mistletoe, a parasitic plant that grows on oak, walnut, cottonwood, and other trees. People who care more about trees than about kissing under mistletoe at Christmas will value this creature, which can be found primarily in the South, coast to coast. Butterflies can also contribute to natural weed control. Many butterfly larvae, such as the West Coast lady, feast on nettles, that bane of Western hikers. Yet, true to nature's way of keeping things in balance, the nettles aren't on anyone's threatened species list.

Butterflies have a fascinating distribution, too. Some, for example the painted lady or the red admiral, are found nationwide; others are found everywhere except for a specific area. It's disappointing that we in the Northwest do not see the monarch, while the rest of the country does. The woodland skipper, though, a Western butterfly, is at home in vacant lots in downtown Seattle. Other butterflies limit their areas to the West or the East, and some are so specific they are found only in a very restricted area. The Hermes copper is found only in the vicinity of San Diego, California, where encroaching development and urban sprawl is threatening the survival of the species.

Because butterflies generally need warm weather and sunshine to be able to fly, it stands to reason that the South has more butterfly species than the North. Some species, however, have adapted to cold weather and are found only in Arctic regions on all the continents that surround the North Pole. The Greenland sulphur has even adapted to life in Greenland. Because of our cloudy days, western Washington may be the most butterfly-deprived area of the country, as you can see from the table at the end of this section. Still, some have adapted even to this climate, but they are so specific to the west slope of the Cascade Mountains that I have not included them, as they are primarily of local interest. Another butterfly, the Uncompahgre butterfly, occurs only in the San Juan Mountains of southwest Colorado. They are not included in the table, either.

Most butterfly fanciers will say, "Yes, yes, we know they are fascinating and mostly beneficial, but you're missing the point! Butterflies are beautiful!" And so they are. People often hang translucent butterfly images in their windows to refract sunlight, but almost nothing can surpass the beauty of a butterfly in motion on a bright sunny day. As I was waiting for a bus one sunny July day, a yellow-and-black swallowtail danced by, and my spirits danced with it.

Butterflies appear erratic in flight, but everything they do has a purpose—to survive and propagate their species. Like other wild creatures, unless butterflies have the plants they need for their life cycle and unless the climate is right for them, they will die. That's why gardening for butterflies is ideally suited for wildlife and native plant gardeners. By re-creating the local ecosystem, or coming as close to it as you can, you will attract some of the earth's most beautiful creatures. Midwesterners can transform their lawns into meadows or mini meadows of native wildflowers and grasses and enjoy the aerobatics of butterflies among bright flowers and gently waving grasses. By giving up their lawns, Southern Californians can provide habitat for the California dogface, which has a much prettier name that is more descriptive of this brilliant orange-and-black insect: flying pansy. Other Southern California butterflies include San Emigdio blue, Hermes copper, Avalon hairstreak, orange-veined blue. Throughout the desert Southwest, people might be fortunate enough to attract and help preserve the Rita blue or the small blue, two desert species that are often mistaken for each other.

Wildlife gardeners together can help to assure that other local, native butterflies do not suffer the fate of the xerces blue, which became extinct in 1943. In memory of it, the Xerces Society, a worldwide group, is devoted to conserving rare insects by recognizing and protecting their natural habitats. For information on butterflies specific to your area, this group or the Audubon Society are good sources.

As with most other wild creatures, the key to attracting butterflies is to provide the food, shelter, and water they can use to complete their life cycle. You can do this with any size garden, from acres of meadow to a window box. Butterflies can detect their food sources from miles away and will fly to them over considerable distances. Even in a city, you can put plants for butterflies in a balcony pot or a window box, and as long as they have the other ingredients close by, they will find your garden and stay, delighting you for years to come. Plate 11 (following page 116) shows a swallowtail butterfly among pansies in a planter box. Even if you live in a small apartment or condominium, you can do something similar. In return, butterflies will contribute to the survival of the planet by pollinating plants, not only garden plants, but native plants in danger of extinction.

To attract butterflies to your habitat, first find out which species are native to your area. The table at the end of this section is only a very partial list of the more than 7,000 species of butterfly in North America. Some butterflies thrive only at certain altitudes; others can survive only at low altitudes. Some live in deserts, while still other butterflies need wetlands. Some are tropical; some are arctic. Learning about them is a delightful discovery.

Some butterflies are fragile and will not survive outside their native habitat; others are adaptable and thrive anywhere their basic needs are met. The wonderful monarch, the only butterfly to make lengthy annual migrations, can be found almost everywhere and asks for little more than milkweed (*Asclepias* spp.) and dogbane (*Apocynum* spp.) as host plants, and nectar plants.

When you have an idea of which butterflies appear in your area, consider their needs at each of the four stages in their life cycle: egg, larva, pupa, and adult. A female may lay hundreds of eggs in her short life span, often one at a time, separately, on the undersides of leaves where the eggs will be as inconspicuous as possible. With instinctive foresight, she lays this egg on a plant that the caterpillar can begin to eat immediately when it emerges from the egg. Caterpillars continue eating constantly until they reach their full growth, usually in about two weeks. If you want butterflies to come to your habitat and make their homes there, or to return year after year, plant the host plants, those the butterfly larvae can eat.

If you're concerned that caterpillars will decimate some of your plants, you can depend on nature's pest management. Birds find caterpillars (except for the monarch) very tasty, and the birds you welcome to your garden will prevent the caterpillars from becoming a problem.

On the other hand, caterpillars can also be an effective means to control pest plants. For example, the Milbert's tortoiseshell caterpillar, question mark caterpillar, red admiral caterpillar, and West Coast lady caterpillar, all eat stinging nettles (*Urtica*).

After about two weeks, the full-sized larva begins to spin a casing around itself. This silk casing hardens into the chrysalis. The chrysalis may be camouflaged to look like a leaf, a wart on a stem, a twig, a bit of bark, or even bird droppings. Inside the chrysalis, the larva metamorphoses into a butterfly. After about another two weeks, the chrysalis becomes transparent, and the butterfly emerges.

In their adult stage, butterflies need shrubs for protection and flowers for nectar to feed on. They also need sunny places, animal droppings, and mud. Butterflies need sunny places because they are cold-blooded; their body temperature rises and falls with the air temperature. When the air is cold, they're cold. Unless they're warm, they can't fly or gather nectar, establish territories, mate, lay eggs, and carry out all their other activities.

Besides nectar, which has no salt, butterflies depend on animal droppings and mud for the salts they need to round out their diets. For the mainstay of their diet, nectar, adult butterflies need flowers that produce nectar. Most butterfly books state that, in general, butterflies can use only flat-topped flowers, preferably the single kinds. For these butterflies, the best kinds are daisies, dandelions, black-eyed Susans, and others in the family Compositae. Their flat tops make it easy for a butterfly to land securely while it eats. Other butterflies, however, have much different needs. Milbert's tortoiseshell, for example, feeds exclusively on nettles, both as a caterpillar and as an adult.

Each species of butterfly is particular about the plants it will feed on or lay its eggs on. The monarch, for example, lays its eggs on milkweed only. Feeding on milkweed makes the monarch taste so bad to its predators that the viceroy has imitated the monarch's coloring to fool birds into thinking it's a monarch. The viceroy, though, has a black band across its wings. The following table lists some of the more common butterflies nationwide and the plants they need, both as caterpillars and as adults.

Notice that neither butterfly bush (*Buddleia davidii*) nor Queen

Anne's lace (*Daucus carota*) is listed. Both plants are on Washington State lists of plants to watch out for. They appear to be in danger of colonizing in natural areas. To be sure you're not planting something you'll regret later, check with your local native plant society or cooperative extension service to be sure it or another plant does not appear on a similar list in your area. The extension can also help you select native flowers that attract the butterflies native to your specific area. Even in the New York City borough of Manhattan, the Cornell University Extension (Midtown) can help you with plants to attract butterflies and other wildlife, as can the Brooklyn Botanic Garden and the New York Botanical in the Bronx.

The tables in this chapter list the range of the butterfly first, to help you locate the butterflies that might be attracted to your garden. It seems rather pointless for me, for example, to try to attract a monarch butterfly—they're not found on the Northwest Pacific Coast. The definitions of parts of the contiguous United States might be confusing to some people. By the "East" I mean the area east of the Mississippi River. The "West" includes the thirteen Western states. The "Midwest" is the area between the Mississippi and the Rocky Mountains. The "South" includes the area from coast to coast that lies or would lie south of the old Mason-Dixon line. The "Southeast" is the Old South, below the Mason-Dixon line and east of the Mississippi. The "Southwest" includes Texas, Arizona, New Mexico, and Southern California, with the southern parts of Colorado, Utah, and Nevada. Coastal terms refer to those states who form part of the coast, as Florida, Alabama, Mississippi, Louisiana, and Texas are "Gulf States."

The second column lists the butterfly, followed by its larval plants in the third column, and its nectar plants in the fourth column. The listed plants do not by any means exhaust the plants that may attract the butterfly.

Common Butterflies and Their Foods

Range	Butterfly	Larval Plants	Nectar Plants
nationwide	American painted lady	everlastings (*Anaphalis*	anise hyssop (*Agastache foeniculum*), asters (*Aster* spp.), bee balm (*Monarda* spp.)
	atlantis fritillary	violets	meadow flowers
	gray hairstreak	corn (*Zea mays*), oak, cotton (*Gossypium* spp.), strawberry (*Fragaria* spp.), mint (Lamiaceae)	anise hyssop (*Agastache foeniculum*), asters (*Aster* spp.), bee balm (*Monarda* spp.), heliotrope [Cherry pie] (*Heliotropium arborescens*)
	mourning cloak	willow, elm, hackberry	milkweed (*Asclepias* spp.) [Also known as butterfly weed]
	painted lady	globe thistle (*Echinops exaltatus*), mallows (Malvaceae)	asters (*Aster* spp.), globe thistle (*Echinops exaltatus*)
	red admiral	nettles (*Urtica*)	anise hyssop (*Agastache foeniculum*), asters (*Aster* spp.), milkweed (*Asclepias* spp.) [Also known as butterfly weed]
	spring azure	dogwood (*Cornus* spp.), viburnum, ceanothus (*Ceanothus* spp.), blueberries (*Vaccinium* spp.,), meadowsweet (*Spiraea* spp.)	milkweed (*Asclepias* spp.) [butterfly weed]; lilac (*Syringa vulgaris*)

Common Butterflies and Their Foods, continued

Range	Butterfly	Larval Plants	Nectar Plants
nationwide, except Atlantic and Pacific Coasts	Gorgone crescentspot	sunflowers (*Helianthus* spp.), ragweed (*Ambrosia trifida*)	goldenrod (*Solidago* spp.)
nationwide, except Northwest and northern New England	common checkered skipper	mallows (*Malva* spp.), hollyhock (*Althaea* spp.)	hollyhock (*Althaea* spp.), hibiscus (*Hibiscus*), mallows (*Malva* spp.)
nationwide, except most of Florida	common sulphur	clovers (*Trifolium* spp.)	clover (*Trifolium* spp.), milkweed (*Asclepias* spp.) [butterfly weed]
nationwide, except Washington State	checkered white	turnips, cabbages, bee plant (*Cleome*)	aster (*Aster* spp.), milkweed (*Asclepias* spp.) [butterfly weed]

Range	Butterfly	Larval Plants	Nectar Plants
nationwide, except Pacific Northwest	monarch	milkweed (*Asclepias* spp.)	milkweed (*Asclepias* spp.) [Also known as butterfly weed],goldenrod (*Solidago* spp.); joe-pye weed (*Eupatorium purpureum*); lilac (*Syringa vulgaris*)
	orange sulphur	alfalfa, clover (*Trifolium* spp.)	alfalfa
nationwide, except Pacific Coast	brown elfin	blueberries (*Vacinium*), bearberry (*Arcostaphylos urva-ursi*), azalea, California lilac (*Ceanothus* spp.), salal (*Gaultheria shalon*), apples, madrona (*Arbutus*)	bearberry or kinnikinnick (*Arcostaphylos urva-ursi*)
	pearly crescentspot	aster (*Aster* spp.)	thistle (*Cirsium*), aster (*Aster* spp.), fleabanes
	tiger swallowtail	cottonwood, birch, ash (*Fraxinus* spp.), tulip tree (*Liriodendron tulipifera*)	lilac, honeysuckle, milkweed (*Asclepias* spp.) [butterfly weed]
	viceroy	willows, poplars, aspen, apple, cherry, plum	goldenrod (*Solidago* spp.), milkweed (*Asclepias* spp.) [butterfly weed], joe-pye weed (*Eupatorium purpureum*)

Common Butterflies and Their Foods, continued

Range	Butterfly	Larval Plants	Nectar Plants
nationwide, except Pacific Coast and Florida	silver-spotted skipper	wisteria (*Wisteria*), locusts (*Gleditsia* spp.), beans (*Phaseolus* spp.)	zinnias (*Zinnia* spp.), honeysuckle (*Lonicera* spp.), milkweed, (*Asclepias* spp.) [butterfly weed], joe-pye weed (*Eupatorium purpureum*)
nationwide, except the Rockies	buckeye	plantain (*Plantago* spp.), stonecrop (*Dudleya* spp.)	aster (*Aster* spp.), coreopsis (*Coreopsis* spp.), globe thistle (*Echinops exaltatus*)
nationwide, except S. California, S. Florida	roadside skipper	Kentucky bluegrass (*Poa pratensis*), bent grass (*Agrostis*), Bermuda grass (*Cynodon dactylon*)	ground ivy
nationwide, except far Southwest, Gulf Coast, Pacific Northwest	coral hairstreak	plums, wild cherries, western serviceberry	milkweed (*Asclepias* spp.) [butterfly weed], bee plant
nationwide, except extreme Southeast	great spangled fritillary	violets	black-eyed Susan (*Rudbeckia* spp.), milkweed (*Asclepias* spp.) [butterfly weed], thistles (*Cirsium*)

Range	Butterfly	Larval Plants	Nectar Plants
East	dusted skipper	beard grass (*Andropogon scoparius*)	blackberry, strawberry, and clover (*Trifolium* spp.).
	eastern tailed blue	clover (*Trifolium* spp.), beans, wild peas	clover (*Trifolium* spp.)
	golden-banded skipper	hog peanut (*Amphicarpa*)	hollyhock, ironweed, buttonbush
	little yellow	senna, clover (*Trifolium* spp.)	clover (*Trifolium* spp.)
East and Great Plains	question mark	nettles, hackberries	rotting fruit, milkweed (*Asclepias* spp.) [butterfly weed]
Northeast	Diana	violets	thistles (*Cirsium*), dogbane (*Apocynum* spp.)
	northern metalmark	bush sunflower, mule fat (*Baccharis glutinosa*)	sunflowers
	white admiral	birches, willows, poplars	aphid honeydew, flowers

Common Butterflies and Their Foods, continued

Range	Butterfly	Larval Plants	Nectar Plants
Northeast and northern Great Plains	prairie ringlet	grasses	grasses
Northeast, except New England	hickory hairstreak	hickories, ashes	dogwood, milkweed (*Asclepias* spp.) [butterfly weed], Queen Anne's lace
South	Eufala skipper	grasses	asters (*Aster* spp.)
	great purple hairstreak	mistletoe	mistletoe
	Gulf fritillary	Passionflower vines	lantana (*Lantana* spp.), impatiens, thistle (*Cirsium* spp.)
	red-banded hairstreak	dwarf sumac, croton	sumac flowers
South and Southwest	sleepy orange	senna (*Cassia* spp.), clover (*Trifolium* spp.)	clover (*Trifolium* spp.)
Southeast	clouded skipper	various wild grasses (*Andropogon, Stenotaphrum secundatum*), corn (*Zea mays*)	various wild grasses (*Andropogon, Stenotaphrum secundatum*)

Range	Butterfly	Larval Plants	Nectar Plants
	king's hairstreak	horse sugar buds, flame azalea	chinkapin flowers
	red dusted skipper	beard grass (*Andropogon scoparius*)	blackberry, strawberry, and clover (*Trifolium* spp.).
West	dotted blue	wild buckwheat	wild buckwheat
	woodland skipper	grasses	everlasting (*Antennaria, Anaphalis*)
The West, except the Pacific Coast	Edith's checkerspot	Indian paintbrush, plantain	various flowers
West and Midwest	Milbert's tortoiseshell	nettles (*Urtica*)	goldenrod (*Solidago* spp.), thistle (*Cirsium* spp.), Marigolds (*Tagetes* spp.), asters (*Aster* spp.)
West and Great Plains (except South-west and South)	greenish blue	clover (*Trifolium* spp.)	bistort (*Polygonum bistortoides*), asters (*Aster* spp.), white clover (*Trifolium repens*)
Great Plains	Edwards' fritillary	violets (*Viola* spp.)	thistle (*Cirsium*), coneflower (*Rudbeckia lanciniata*)

Attracting Bees

Of all the pollinators, bees, butterflies, and hummingbirds, the major pollinators are bees. Some plants cannot reproduce unless pollinators carry pollen from male plants to female plants, or from the male parts of some plants to their female parts. The female plants then make seeds that become food for birds or are scattered by wind to become next season's flowers.

Pollinators are a vital part of the agricultural economy as well, because without them carrying pollen among the flowers of our fruit trees, we would have no apples, pears, peaches, plums, etc. I can't imagine a summer without peach juice running down my chin or autumn without a crisp, tasty apple to crunch on.

Wildlife gardeners can make our contribution to agriculture by ensuring that we provide for bees in our gardens. We can do this by planting native perennial wildflowers, flowering shrubs, and flowering trees for bees to get nectar from. Some gardeners also set aside areas of their gardens for annuals that are known to attract pollinators of all types.

Besides these food sources, bees need shelter from predators and places to nest and mate. They need water, and some bees need mud as a nest-building material. Other bees must have leaf material, so don't worry if some of your plants have small pieces munched from their leaves. As long as the plant is otherwise healthy, it can spare a few parts for bees' nests. Bees also nest in snags and deadfall, so if you have dead wood on your property, the bees will make a home in small holes.

Bees are entertaining creatures, too. Our property is fortunate to have a nest of mason bees underground, in the remains of an old alder stump over which a sword fern has taken root. These small bees have black heads and wide black stripes around the thorax. We don't disturb them; we just let them go about their business. Often I have watched them dart about, gathering pollen and nectar from a fireweed flower, then from a Japanese anemone, and back again.

When we began the garden, we wanted something in bloom all year around. Winters in the Puget Sound region do not have the extremely long, cold winters of other places in this latitude, but the days are short and cloudy and damp, much like England. After some research, we planted flowering shrubs, and now we do have flowers during every month of the year. At the time, we couldn't predict that every February bumblebees gather nectar from the *Pieris japonica* by our front porch.

We don't know where those bumblebees nest, but we're always happy to see them. Their cheerful activity brightens winter days and promises us that spring will come this year, too.

Life in Your Backyard

This planet, the human life support system, depends on every sort of plant and animal that exists, the cute and the ugly, the visible and the microscopic, creatures that move on more than four legs and others that move on fewer than two. Wildlife sanctuary gardeners encourage animals to take up residence on "our" property or stop by for a snack on their way to somewhere else.

The primary food source for wildlife is native vegetation. As we have seen, you can incorporate native plants into your garden, but the number of wild visitors to your garden may exceed these food supplies. Normal growth cycles limit seeds, berries, and fruits to late summer or autumn, flowers to spring and summer (normally). During the other times of the year, animals that depend on these food sources need you to supplement the available foods with bird seed, corn, fruit holders, and suet.

No matter where you live, there will be several reputable sources for seeds, suet, and corn, besides other types of food for the wildlife in your area. If you have a specialty store in your area or another source of information, you may want to consider selecting food for each species of animal you wish to attract. Some experts on bird feeding, for example, recommend against the mixed seeds that include both millet and black sunflower seed.

How much feeding you do and what kinds of animals you feed will depend on your situation, your budget, and your personal preferences. In a wildlife garden, as in natural areas, there will be competition for food. I've watched while a feisty sparrow keeps all the other sparrows, nuthatches, house finches, and chickadees away from a platform feeder with room for a dozen small birds. And when the crow feasts on suet, other birds remain at a respectful distance. If you feed birds, you will feed squirrels, unless there are no squirrels in your vicinity. They are clever and resourceful, and few bird feeders are truly squirrelproof.

If you garden for wildlife, you'll have several signs when you're successful:

- The heron dines on your fish.
- The hawk snatches a small bird.
- The peregrine nesting on the urban cliffside of a skyscraper grabs a pigeon.
- The snakes take care of your mouse problem.
- The moles make bumps in the ground.
- Your cold compost pile swarms with sow bugs.

All of these events prove that nature has arrived. By our standards, reared as we are on Bambi and Thumper, these signs are not pleasant, but how else are wild creatures to get the food they need to sustain themselves?

And, ultimately, to sustain us?

Chapter 5

The
Backyard
Wetland
Sanctuary

Besides food and shelter, animals need
a reliable, year-round supply of water. So important is this need that
most programs that certify backyard wildlife habitats require you to have
a supply of water. No matter whether you are feeding birds on your balcony or setting aside acres of land, you can provide water for the creatures you attract to your sanctuary. You can make some sort of beautiful
and enjoyable water feature to fit your situation, from a simple birdbath
to a water garden that simulates a natural wetland.

In general, a wetland is land that is saturated with water at least part
of the year. Drainage is often poor, and plants have adapted to growing
with their roots in water most or all of the time. Wetland ecosystems have
an interdependent relationship of plants and animals adapted to wet
conditions. Some wetlands are underwater all year; others dry out periodically. There's enough variety in wetlands that you can find a model
for your backyard wetland. The illustration on the next page shows an
underwater ecosystem. At flood times, the water may be high enough to
affect the terrestrial plant community.

You can make a pond or a bog, large or small. For gardening
purposes, a bog is shallow and filled with soil and decaying plant
matter—it can also partially dry out during dry spells—such as western

Underwater Ecosystem

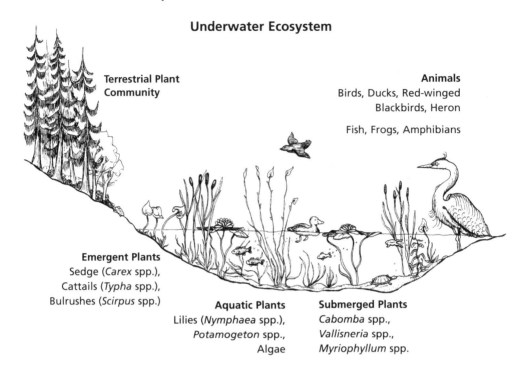

Terrestrial Plant Community

Animals
Birds, Ducks, Red-winged Blackbirds, Heron

Fish, Frogs, Amphibians

Emergent Plants
Sedge (*Carex* spp.),
Cattails (*Typha* spp.),
Bulrushes (*Scirpus* spp.)

Aquatic Plants
Lilies (*Nymphaea* spp.),
Potamogeton spp.,
Algae

Submerged Plants
Cabomba spp.,
Vallisneria spp.,
Myriophyllum spp.

Underwater, another type of ecosystem provides for the well-being of all its inhabitants, whether or not they live beneath the water's surface.

Washington's annual summer drought—but the pond has water in it year-round.

If you're gardening on a city balcony, you can put in a birdbath. You might also consider growing a water lily in a lined tub or barrel or having a basin with a trickle of water running into it—as long as it doesn't overflow and bother your downstairs neighbors.

The value of what you do, on whatever scale, can hardly be overstated. All creatures need accessible water. The United States has lost more than half its wetlands since the country began, according to some official government estimates, because of development, agriculture, and erosion of the coastline. In western Washington, a famously damp area, approximately 90 percent of wetlands has been and is being lost.

It's not surprising, really. Attitudes to wetlands, as we now call these areas, are deeply rooted in the European psyche as mysterious, even evil, places where dangerous creatures lurk ready to devour us. The fen, the swamp, the bog—all have appeared in popular literature as places where people vanish in the fog or sink into the ground, never to be seen again. Reread Sir Arthur Conan Doyle's *The Hound of the Baskervilles* for a hair-raising story of the hound from hell chasing people across boggy ground through a fog. Since the discovery of a certain type of mosquito as the cause of malaria and the realization that mosquitoes breed in stagnant water, the wetland has been seen as an unhealthy place for humans, which should be drained as a matter of public health.

In the South, the wetlands have been feared as places of danger. Frightening accounts such as the botanist John Bartram's contribute to our terror of the swamp. While on a plant-hunting expedition through the South, Bartram (1699–1777) awoke to find himself being attacked by an alligator that had crawled out of the water to feast—on him. He fought off the attack and spent the rest of the night uneasily, until light came and he was able to move on—not to leave the swamp, however, but to continue his explorations.

Modern entertainment media contribute to this fear of the swamp by setting horror movies in swampy areas where vines come alive to strangle the unwary, and ferocious bugs grow to the size of cars. For some people, being terrified is great fun, but it underscores the sense that wetlands are useless, awful places.

Ironically, as the nation's wetlands rapidly disappear, they are being recognized for their value to humans. Natural wetlands are valuable in many ways. They are vital to coastal fishing. As just one example, the life cycle of salmon is dependent on interior wetlands. (The precise term is *riparian habitats*.) These fish spawn and hatch and grow in rivers and streams (also considered to be a type of wetland), then migrate to the open ocean where they spend their adult lives. When the salmon are ready, they return to begin the cycle all over again. When they spawn and die, they become food for bald eagles, bears, and other animals, who nest by the hundreds where salmon have spawned, just as they have done for thousands of years.

Wetlands, both on the coast and in the interior of the country, are essential for millions of waterfowl, other birds, mammals, and reptiles for breeding, nesting, feeding, and hiding from predators. Of the 564 plant and animal species listed as threatened or endangered in the United States, more than one-third use wetland habitats during some part of their life cycle. (For more information on the value of wetlands, check out this URL sponsored by the Environmental Protection Agency: www.epa.gov/owow/wetlands.)

Wetlands are crucial to maintaining the water level of some watersheds and serve as natural reservoirs and groundwater recharge areas. As rain falls or floods come, the wetlands collect the water, then filter it gradually as it sinks into the earth to pool in vast underground lakes called aquifers, from which come some municipal water supplies. Wetlands are important in protecting the quantity and quality of the groundwater we use for drinking. Where reservoirs are built to collect drinking water from streams and rivers, the resulting wetland filters the water and helps sediments to settle out so that by the time the water enters our water supplies, it's safe to drink.

Constructed wetlands are a relatively new means of treating wastewater from our sewer systems. After building a pond and setting out native wetland plants, the wastewater is diverted into it from the wastewater treatment plants. A natural filtration process takes place in which microbes and plants consume the nutrients in the wastewater. The water, rendered much cleaner, seeps through the soil and enters the groundwater, which flows beneath the surface of the earth.

In addition, wetlands provide resources for diverse populations of plant and animal life, a boon to recreational fishers and bird-watchers alike. (For more detailed information, refer to chapter 8 for the URL on this topic.)

You may not want to have people fishing—even catch-and-release—in your backyard, but even a small wetland habitat can welcome amphibians and fish and serve as a stopover for migrating waterfowl. Each spring, for several years, a pair of mallard ducks has found our ponds and settled in for a few days before taking off for their nesting grounds. Year-round, frogs have made their homes there and entertained us with their serenades, and birds amuse us with their antics as they wash the grit and dust from their feathers. The photos opposite show our lower pond in early spring, about March. Most of the plants have not yet broken dormancy, but the garden is colorful with yellow daffodils and white

A backyard wildlife wetland can be larger as ours is.

Or smaller, as is this pond in another wildlife sanctuary garden.

Osmanthus delavayi (a flowering shrub) and the pink thundercloud flowering plum in the background. At this time of year I enjoy the reflections in the water before the water lilies have begun to send up their leaves.

As these photos show, however, a water garden does not have to be large to be effective and inviting to wildlife. The small pond is home to a couple of goldfish and at least one frog, who shyly stayed out of sight while we were there.

One of my favorite places is the marsh a couple of blocks from our house. Roughly three acres in size, it's a beautiful sight in summer. Douglas's spiraea blooms with fuzzy pink blossoms reminiscent of lilac flowers. Red-winged blackbirds, mallard ducks, and evening grosbeaks nest there, and occasionally the great blue heron visits. Frogs announce spring every year. Not every suburban area is fortunate enough to have a wetland, even one the developers bisected with a street.

Backyard swimming pools contribute to the loss of wetlands, because natural wetland areas are often drained and streams are diverted from their natural courses to provide water for urban areas and their swimming pools. The environmental damage done by lawns may well be equalled by the damage done by a swimming pool. In addition, the pool must be chlorinated and otherwise chemically treated, making it poisonous to wildlife. If you want to make a backyard wetland habitat, however, you might consider filling in the pool, constructing sloping sides so wild creatures can climb out, and turning it into a wetland.

When constructing your backyard wetland habitat, as with the terrestrial garden, you will have the most success and satisfaction from using plants grown in your area. These plants have adapted to the particular combination of geology, rainfall, and temperatures in your area. For example, a plant that originates here in the Seattle area will not be completely satisfactory in the Midwest, where it rains in the summer. It will be accustomed to drying out in the summer. Likewise, a plant advertised as native to North America that originates in Georgia, although in the same climate zone, will not be satisfactory in Washington because it will be accustomed to getting rain in the summer and to living with more summer humidity.

Another reason not to import wetland plants from another area is the chance we take of introducing a plant that will damage the wetland ecology. Purple loosestrife (*Lythrum salicaria*), reed canary grass (*Phalaris arundinacea*), hybrid cattail (*Typha* x *glauca*), tamarisks (*Tamarix chinensis*, *T. parviflora*, and *T. ramosissima*), glossy buckthorn (*Rhamnus frangula*), and water hyacinth (*Eichhornia crassipes*) are all invasive and will overrun a wetland. Although some of these plants originally had value for horticultural or other purposes, such as their tolerance to fertilizers and salts, the damage they have done to natural areas has long since turned them from treasure to pest.

Unfortunately, by planting some exotic plants, even natives from another part of North America, we defeat our purpose—to make a haven for wildlife. If our garden plants escape into the wild (and they will, with the help of our bird friends), they may very well overrun natural areas and drive out species of plants that wildlife must have to survive.

Of course, not everyone has the space to model a wetland, but every little bit helps, and whatever you can do, as I've said before, is far better than doing nothing. For many people, a birdbath may fit their needs.

Birdbaths

Birdbaths are the simplest and least expensive means of providing water, and they're a delight to have. You can have one or several and place them anywhere, near a window so you can watch without being seen, near your favorite indoor or outdoor sitting area. You can place them where the birds will think they're alone, but even if birds see you, if you sit still, pretty soon the birds will accept your being there and come anyway.

Putting a birdbath near a children's play space, though, will frighten the birds off. Also make sure there is cover nearby so they can fly to safety when they're startled or when cats and other predators make an appearance.

Not only will birdbaths attract birds, but other small animals will find them, too. Squirrels will play and squabble with each other. Perhaps few things are as comical as two squirrels debating ownership of a small pool of water. Butterflies and bees will also appreciate a drink now and then. The birdbath on the next page shows how water was incorporated into a small condominium yard.

On a balcony, a birdbath works well because you can easily clean it and fill it without worrying about spilling great quantities of water. And the weight of the water and the bath combined won't be so great as to cause concern in your landlord or building superintendent.

Birdbaths come in many styles, so you can easily find one that suits your purpose and aesthetic sense, from simple plastic to ornate stone carvings to lightweight copper birdbaths that are almost works of art. They may consist of the basin only or include a basin and a miniature waterfall arrangement. If you opt for a basin, you can set it on the ground or balcony floor, or you can put it on a pedestal.

You can also make your own from garbage can lids, potted plant saucers, or any similar container. You can fill brightly colored plastic children's play saucers, the kind kids use for sliding in winter. The container should be textured to give birds a footing. If you use something slippery, line it with pebbles so they can get a foothold while they're bathing. Stone, concrete, or ceramic saucers work well, too. Just be sure the container has a basic saucer shape. It should be shallow, no deeper than three inches, and have gently sloping sides for a gradual increase in depth. Small birds like to walk into the water to a comfortable depth for drinking or bathing. If you prefer, you can set the container on any sort of pedestal—an unused plant stand, a few bricks stacked to the desired height, or an arrangement of pipes—or, you can set one on a stump for a rustic effect.

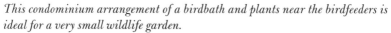

This condominium arrangement of a birdbath and plants near the birdfeeders is ideal for a very small wildlife garden.

Japanese gardens can inspire you to a double-duty birdbath. Place a shallow basin (three inches to four inches deep) with sloping sides on the floor or ground. Place a larger stone, perhaps two or three feet tall, next to the basin and lay a bamboo rod across the stone, sloping downward so water will drip or trickle from the rod onto the basin. The simplest way to keep a constant trickle is to connect the rod to a garden hose and let it trickle in only when you are there to enjoy or monitor it.

Another method would be to buy a half barrel, line it with a sturdy bag, and fill it with water. You can plant a water lily here, and place a submersible pump in it, then pipe the water to the stone. If you do this, be sure to consult with an electrical supply house for a ground fault interrupt (GFI). By code you must have this device for safety for anything outdoors. It trips immediately to interrupt the circuit of power and protect you or the animals from electrocution. One drawback to using a barrel is the danger the barrel may present to birds and other small animals that hop into the barrel for a bath or a drink and can't get out again.

I don't recommend making anything out of concrete if you are using it for an outdoor water feature. The concrete must be completely cured before it can be used as a water garden. This could take six months to a year. Concrete also does not give with changes in temperature. If you live where winters are hard, and the ground heaves in the cold, it may crack. Even here, where winters are mild, so much moisture is in the ground that very low temperatures freeze the water in the ground and cause it to swell in the winter.

If you live where water freezes in winter, you can buy an electric water heater that will keep the water warm. Some of these can be set to turn off during higher daytime temperatures. However, I'd recommend keeping your arrangement simple. Except where winters are very hard, you might switch the containers every morning. Put the frozen ones where they will thaw and replace them with basins of warm water. Another method is to pour boiling water onto the ice to thaw it and replace the ice chunks with warm water.

Cleaning is also important year-round. Keep the birdbaths filled with fresh water and scrub them as often as needed to get rid of algae and droppings.

Backyard Wetlands and Water Gardens

A water garden is to a backyard wetland habitat as a lawn is to a meadow. The primary differences between a water garden and a backyard wetland habitat are the purposes for which you build it and the amount of maintenance required after you've built it. A backyard wetland is like the wildlife sanctuary garden; it is built as a haven for aquatic wildlife and birds, and for people to enjoy, too. Once established, your backyard wetland carries on by itself, without much intervention from you.

A water garden, on the other hand, is usually built for a purpose other than to provide water for wildlife, such as to grow water lilies or to keep koi. A water garden takes considerable work to ensure that the water plants—lilies and irises—bloom successfully. They need regular fertilizing and repotting once a year. Repotting means removing the water-logged pots from the pond, dumping out the old soil, dividing the plants, and replacing them in new soil and putting the pots back into the water. (Fortunately, you don't need many water lilies; each lily may spread its leaves out in a circle with a diameter of six feet.)

Koi fanciers prevent wildlife from getting into koi ponds. Frogs may bring in diseases and eat young koi. Herons and raccoons will eat koi for dinner—and breakfast and lunch, if they get the chance. Keeping koi and having a backyard wetland seem to me to be mutually contradictory—but then, before I understood that what I really wanted to do was to have a simulated wetland, I had lost all of my koi to predators.

If you have even a small lot, you can simulate a mini wetland and do a big favor for creatures that cannot speak for themselves. A backyard wetland provides for the needs of terrestrial wildlife and is itself a habitat for water-based plants and wild creatures such as fish, amphibians, and turtles. In some places, it's also a habitat for water moccasins, crocodiles, and 'gators. If these creatures are part of your environment, I'd suggest consulting with local wildlife experts before you begin to put in a backyard wetland habitat. Endangering you or your family goes counter to the idea of a sanctuary garden.

Despite the rewards of a backyard wetland, some people balk at creating an artificial wetland on the grounds that it wastes water, or attracts mosquitoes, or is too much work. But these concerns are unnecessary.

Wasting Water?

Rightly recognizing that water is too precious a resource to waste, gardeners everywhere have turned to xeriscaping, gardening without water or with the least amount of water possible. Building a backyard wetland is not incompatible with xeriscaping, however. Xeriscaping speaks primarily to wasting water—using water to maintain exotic flower beds and lawns. Using water for a backyard wetland is a far different thing than setting sprinklers to run for hours on a lawn or filling a swimming pool.

Every living creature, even in the desert, needs water. Desert animals seek out seeps and springs and have adapted to periods of drought. I live in a part of the country famous for its constant drizzle, but in summer we have two months when it doesn't rain at all. Some native plants have adapted to this annual summer drought. For those that have not adapted, that need water year-round, a mini wetland provides much-needed water for creatures that would otherwise die.

Butterflies and frogs will also benefit from the water. Some amphibians are adapted to periods without water, but amid the widespread alarm at the decline in frog populations, providing a source of clean water may be something a gardener can do to stave off the loss of local frog and butterfly species.

We have also found that the backyard wetland cuts down on the amount of water we might use in the rest of the garden, for the rhododendrons and nonnative trees. The water garden adds humidity to the air, which the leaves absorb during transpiration.

Attracting Mosquitoes?

Some people fear that a small wetland, especially a bog garden, might become a breeding ground for pesky insects such as mosquitoes. We have not found that to be the case. The ponds attracted mosquitoes' natural predators—birds and frogs. The more mosquitoes we have, apparently, the more of their predators are attracted, also. Everything balances out; birds and frogs are happy, and we are, too.

Too Much Work?

In the beginning, some thirteen years ago, we made more work for ourselves with our water garden than we needed to. We tried to find information on simulating a wetland, which is the kind of water gardening we do now, and there was none. Everything we found told us to scrub the pond every couple of months, to let no algae build up, and keep everything neat and tidy. Algae was the bane of a water gardener's life, and nothing was worse than to let the water garden act like a swamp or marsh.

When we look back on our beginning efforts at water gardening, we have to laugh. We did so much unnecessary work in the early stages. We began by being almost fanatically clean in our approach to water gardening. We worried about algae, vacuumed out gunk with a special water-driven vacuum, picked out blanket weed, raked leaves out in the autumn, and filtered the water—all to keep it clean. Gradually, other things claimed our attention. Little by little, we stopped fussing over the water garden, and guess what? It didn't matter. Fish didn't suddenly float to the top. The water remained clear and clean. The water lilies and pickerelweed bloomed.

We felt guilty about our lack of tidiness. But as we spent less time on the water garden, we found ourselves naturally developing a less finicky attitude. We relaxed. The ponds took care of themselves. Now, for about the last five years, we have not cleaned up. We don't remove fading water lily leaves and blossoms. These provide food and shelter for amphibians and other creatures.

Most water garden books say to locate ponds away from deciduous trees, but our upper pond wraps partially around a bigleaf maple tree, and the lower pond lies close to the cascara. We leave most of the fallen leaves in the ponds, where they decompose and become part of the soft, muddy bottom. In this bottom, fish live and frogs hibernate during the winter. We rake out enough leaves to make the ponds clear, but over time the smaller, upper pond has become more of a bog garden than a pond.

Our backyard wetland has given us much pleasure, from its beauty and from the variety of life it contains. Water lilies, Louisiana irises, and *Iris fulva* bloom continuously from May until frost; grasses move softly in the breeze; and the waterfall gurgles cheerfully. Rushes have taken root around the perimeter. The animals are always a joy; fish glide swiftly and secretly along their mysterious courses; water spiders scamper across the surface; dragonflies flash about in dizzying changes of direction. Underwater snails are busy in their own nearly imperceptible fashion, and shy tadpoles, who have been sunning themselves just below the surface, scoot for cover when we appear.

How a Water Garden Works

Backyard wetland habitats all operate on the same principles. They can be any size larger than the birdbath, from a shallow bog garden to a pond or two or several. They all have similar needs, which may sound complicated but are actually easy to satisfy:

- The water must somehow circulate to remain fresh and to maintain the level of oxygen that can support plant and animal life.

- Some sort of filtering, preferably biological, must be present.

- The sides must slope gradually from the outside inward.

- The ecosystem must balance with a combination of both plants and animals.

To find out how this works, we must look at nature's water gardens, the wetlands, and specifically the inland freshwater marsh. The marsh is perhaps the closest natural model for the backyard wetland habitat. It's a fascinating world, and by understanding its processes we can re-create the wetland on a smaller scale in our own backyards.

First of all, in a marsh, the soil is constantly saturated or flooded. Fresh water continually flows in to compensate for the loss of water through evaporation from the water surface and transpiration through the leaves of water plants.

Like a marsh, a backyard wetland habitat functions well when there is continual circulation of water, when nutrients cycle into the water and out into the atmosphere, when acidity (pH) is maintained at the right balance, and when the saturated soil is capable of sustaining plant life.

The next four sections—"Water Circulation," "Nutrient Cycling," "Acidity," and "Soil"—explain how the natural processes work in the marsh (and in our backyard wetland). If you'd rather just do it, skip these somewhat technical explanations and go straight to "How to Build a Bog Garden," or "How to Build a Water Garden." Either or both can be part of your backyard wetland habitat.

Water Circulation

In both marsh and backyard wetland, water is the "atmosphere" in which everything lives. It controls the cycling of nutrients (food) and their availability to plants and animals; it determines how much oxygen will be present; and it controls pH. Runoff from surrounding land brings nutrients into a marsh. Water flowing out or evaporating removes materials from the marsh.

Rainfall brings in fresh water and replenishes the water levels. Rainfall also adds oxygen to the water. Watch how raindrops bounce on the water surface of a puddle. On a small scale, this is aeration. The continual circulation of fresh water in and old water out keeps the marsh fresh and clean.

In the backyard wetland, rain and runoff from the rest of the yard contribute nutrients and oxygen in the same manner. Unlike the marsh, though, at our place and at yours, there's a gardener who controls the major intake and outflow of water and contributes to the nutrient supply.

Our backyard wetland (see the drawing opposite) consists of two ponds containing about 4,000 gallons of water, which completely circulates between them every two hours. We took advantage of a natural rise in the level of the lot in making an upper pond and a lower pond. The upper pond lies about fifteen feet away from and approximately three feet above the lower pond. The lower pond is an oval shape about twenty by twelve feet; the upper pond, a kidney shape that wraps around the base of a bigleaf maple, is roughly one-third the size of the lower pond.

On the plan you can see that a submerged pump in the lower pond sends water to the upper pond through an underground one-inch pipe.

The overflow from the upper pond flows into the small connecting stream and down, over a small waterfall, back into the lower pond. A trickle of fresh water is piped into the lower pond during the summer to keep the water level constant. In the winter, rainfall is abundant enough to bring up the water level. The circulation is kept up year-round by an electrical pump with a GFI.

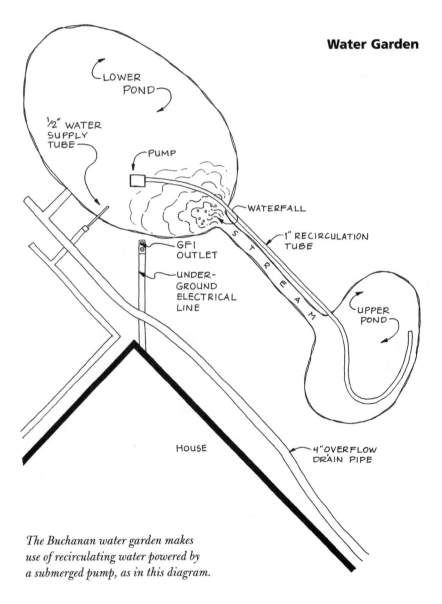

Water Garden

The Buchanan water garden makes use of recirculating water powered by a submerged pump, as in this diagram.

Nutrient Cycling

In a marsh, nutrient cycling is the movement of food among the plants and animals in the backyard wetland. It's who eats whom, or what. The remains of dead plants and animals, together with waste products, are called *detritus.* Other animals eat the detritus, complete their life cycles, die, and are eaten in an unending cycle. The drawing below shows how this works. In this detrital food web you can see who eats and what is eaten. At the top of this web, fish eat insects, fish food, their own fry, and plants. Insects eat other insects and their larvae, and snails and tadpoles eat insects. In turn, they are eaten by fish. Dead plants and animals are

Detrital Food Web

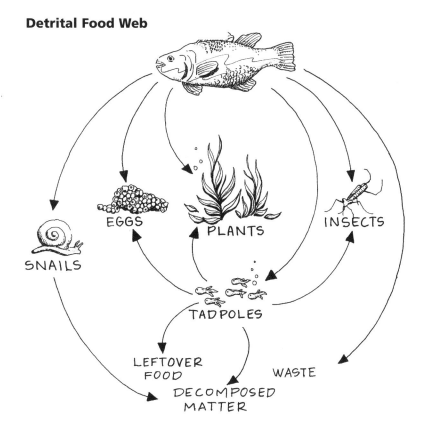

Underwater, as on land, each creature and plant is food for something else, forming a detrital food web.

eaten by snails and tadpoles, who also eat fish waste and leftover fish food. Bacteria convert dead organic matter to available nutrients, some of which are absorbed by plants, which fish eat.

The backyard wetland also depends on the detrital food web to recirculate nutrients among all of the inhabitants. Without this "dining arrangement," toxic substances from decomposing matter would accumulate to undesirable or even lethal levels for the life in the pond. Gardeners can help to establish a detrital food web by putting in the plants and animals that have a part in it. The critters who inhabit the pond then consume the inevitable wastes and dead plant products, and so prevent overpowering the water with toxins.

Our purpose in starting the water garden differed from the beginning from other gardeners' objectives, because we wanted a naturally balanced backyard wetland. Some water gardeners object to introducing fish or other creatures on the grounds that they might eat water lilies. Koi fanciers object to snails on the grounds that they carry diseases that can kill fish. People who want to establish an amphibian environment object to bringing in fish because they eat frog eggs and tadpoles. We experienced none of those problems. Our fish and water lilies remained healthy. The frogs in our garden have the normal complement of four legs and one head, unlike the horrors that we have read about.

Judging from the active pond life, the nutrient balance stays in a healthy range, too. One sure test is to bring a small amount of the accumulation from the bottom and smell it. If there is an odor of rotten eggs, something is out of balance. In our ponds, when I bring up some mud from the bottom, there never has been a bad odor. Nature takes care of its own problems, apparently.

The health of the ponds assures us that natural filtration is working, particularly in nitrification, a vitally important element in the detrital food web. Nitrification is the process of changing nitrogen into the right form to be useful to plants and animals. In nitrification, bacteria convert harmful nitrogen compounds into a form usable by plants, a kind of natural filtration.

In nitrification, two types of bacteria act together in two phases to convert ammonium and other nitrogen compounds into usable nitrate. One bacterium, a microscopic critter called *Nitrosomonas*, breaks down ammonium into nitrate. Another, called *Nitrobacter,* changes nitrite into nitrate. This microbial action is the core of biological filtration. If you buy or build a biological filter, these two bacteria will be present.

You can bring them into the backyard wetland by building a special biological filter, or you can depend on these microbes being naturally present in the detrital food web. We think they must be present in our backyard wetland because the balance of plants and animals appears healthy. If it weren't, it would be quickly noticeable from the fish floating on the water surface and from the smell.

In the beginning, we used filters in the pond, and Dick spent many an afternoon, winter and summer, cleaning the filters. Exactly why he stopped doing it, we don't recall, but we realized that the fish didn't seem to notice, except that we interfered less in the life of the ponds. We realized that the ponds themselves do the filtering.

If you establish a backyard wetland habitat, you will need some sort of filtering system. Either nature will do it, or you will have to set up some sort of biological filter. That sounds more complicated than it is. A biological filter is nothing more than the two microscopic bacteria we mentioned earlier. Whatever holds them will be fine. There are biological filters on the market, also. Check with a local water garden store, or an aquarium store might also be of help.

When we built our pond system, we had the holes excavated in places where the ground was already low, then put down a layer of old carpet (about an inch of newspaper would do as well), followed by a layer of 32 mil reinforced PVC liner. On top of that is a layer of crushed red rock that we bought from a local quarry. Any sort of crushed rock or gravel would do. This rock, we suspect, encourages the presence of nitrifying bacteria in both ponds because they live in the tiny crevices and crannies.

Even after nitrification, nitrates may not be available in sufficient quantities because of the type of soil in which plants are grown, and because nitrates are very mobile. Nitrates don't cling well to soil particles because they both have a negative electrical charge and repel each other. As nitrate moves downward into the soil, some is absorbed by the roots. Some is broken down by microbes into nitrogen (N_2) and nitrous oxide (N_2O) through a process called *denitrification.* This drawing

Water Lily

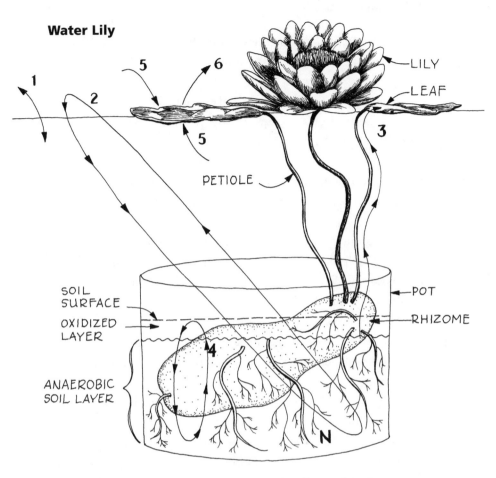

Labels in the diagram:
- LILY
- LEAF
- PETIOLE
- SOIL SURFACE
- OXIDIZED LAYER
- ANAEROBIC SOIL LAYER
- POT
- RHIZOME
- N

This diagram of oxygen circulation through a water lily pot shows how oxygen moves into and out of the water—whether or not plants are in pots.

shows how nutrients and gases cycle through the water. The example uses a potted water lily, but the process is the same for a plant growing in the soil at the bottom, too:

1. Oxygen is exchanged between the water and the air at the water line.

2. In the process of nitrification, atmospheric nitrogen is converted into nitrates usable by the plant, and in the process of denitrification, nitrogen and nitrous oxide escape into the air.

3. Oxygen travels up from the aerobic (oxidized) layer of soil to the leaf and is given off into the atmosphere.

4. Oxygen travels from the oxidized (aerobic) layer of the soil down into the anaerobic layer where the plant converts it into usable carbon dioxide.

5. The leaves take in carbon dioxide from both the water and the air and transpire oxygen into the atmosphere.

In the beginning, the goal is to have enough nitrates for the plants but not too much of a good thing. Too much nitrate turns water to a greenish "pea soup," the infamous "algal bloom." Fortunately, there is an easy biological solution. Totally submerged plants compete with algae for nitrate, with the algae on the losing side if there are enough other plants. These underwater plants are called "oxygenating plants" because, like all plants, they take in carbon dioxide and expel oxygen—even underwater.

In our pond, as a natural soil bottom has developed, submerged oxygenators of various sorts have taken root, courtesy, probably, of the birds. With these underwater plants, and with the waterfall at one end of the pond, we don't need artificial bubblers to provide oxygen underwater. In the winter when the plants are dormant, they are not using oxygen and the hibernating fish use very little. (We keep the ponds open when it freezes to provide oxygen and avoid suffocating the fish.) An additional benefit of submerged plants is to give the fish and visiting ducks something else to munch on besides water lilies. We have to plant new plants from time to time, as they are eaten, but like most gardeners, I don't mind a trip to the nursery. With plenty of plants in the pond, the fish don't eat the water lilies.

Algae is usually considered a problem in most water gardens. Here again, the backyard water habitat differs from most backyard wetlands. Some types of algae—the nitrogen-fixing blue-green algae, for example—are good sources of nitrogen and food for fish, tadpoles, and frogs. As long as the water remains clear, we do not remove algae. Even blanket weed (the long, stringy algae) can be beneficial; tadpoles and fish fry hide from predators in it during the summer, and frogs and fish hibernate in it during the winter. We don't try to eradicate it, but we do control it by raking it out when it looks as if it might take over the pond.

If left to completely take over, algae can rob other plants and underwater wildlife of oxygen. Like most green plants, algae needs sunlight. As water lilies spread their leaves over the surface of the ponds, algae are shaded out. The usual recommended ration of shade to sunlight in a pond is about seventy percent shade. In sunny places in a pond, some algae does not overpower the ponds; instead, it provides extra food for fish.

Acidity

Submerged plants also help to balance the pH of the pond. Acidity or alkalinity is as important to the health of aquatic plants and animals as it is to the terrestrial garden. Using a scale that tests the pH of water, we periodically monitor the health of our backyard wetland. So far (after more than a decade), it has remained in a healthy neutral range of 6.8 to 8.0.

A pH in the range of 6.8 to 8.0 keeps the water habitat healthy and happy by encouraging nitrifying bacteria. After an unusually wet couple of months one summer, the pH of our larger pond tested at 7.4. A month later, after a sudden hot spell with temperatures in the nineties and some new rock work with blue basalt (a basic or alkaline rock formed from basalt), the pH tested at 7.6. The pH can vary from day to day, and the range for contentment in a backyard wetland is fairly wide, so we weren't concerned. The pond's inhabitants seemed happy enough.

We would be concerned if the pH fell below 6.8. In the lower ranges of the pH scale, more hydrogen ions are added. Too much hydrogen contributes to the accumulation of ammonia to toxic levels by providing more hydrogen ions for the nitrogen to combine with. By adding oxygen, submerged plants help to maintain a hospitable chemical balance between toxicity and acidity.

Soil

Nutrients cling to soil particles, and plants absorb nutrients through the cell walls of their microscopic root hairs that wrap around and among the soil particles. The type of soil is as important in the water habitat garden as in the land garden, but when it comes to the underwater world, we have to think differently about soil. For example, organic soil amendments (composted steer manure, leaves, and grass clippings) are highly recommended on land, to loosen the soil and provide more spaces among the soil particles for nutrients to enter into solution with water. In the backyard wetland, though, the decomposition of these amendments can add to the buildup of nitrite and poison the water. Underwater, the heavier the soil, the better. Clay is the most finely textured, with the smallest particles of any type of soil. Each of these particles has more surfaces to which nutrients can bond than a coarser soil type such as sand.

Where the soil surface meets the water, in a plant's container as well as in the soil at the bottom (as in a natural pond), there is a thin aerobic layer, so thin it's measured in millimeters. The aerobic layer contains some oxygen. The drawing on page 125 exaggerates the aerobic (oxidized) layer. Roots of aquatic plants exist almost wholly in the lower, anaero-bic, layer. (*Anaerobic* means "without oxygen.") Anaerobic soils place considerable stress on water plants, some of which have adapted by developing enlarged cells, called *aerenchyma*. These large cells, or air pockets, located throughout the roots and the stems, are extra spaces that can hold more air than normal root cells. Water lilies, for example, have big leaves that absorb lots of oxygen that travels downward through the air pockets. In some aquatic plants, there's even enough air in them for the plants to force it out and create aerobic zones immediately around the roots.

Because plants and animals underwater cannot live without oxygen, the soil must periodically be renewed. In the pond, nature will renew the soil through a combination of means. Organic matter, such as fallen leaves, will decompose, and runoff from the land will carry soils into the pond.

If you combine the water habitat with water gardening (as we do), it is better to grow the water lilies or other water plants such as irises in pots. If you grow these plants in the bottom of the pond, or allow them to "jump" their pots so that they root themselves in the bottom of the pond, it will be difficult to control their growth and prevent them from taking over the available space. Water lilies in particular are vigorous growers, but water irises are not wimpy, either. If you have to uproot them from the bottom you run a risk, depending on how you set up your water garden, of possibly damaging the pond liner. Certainly, uprooting them will disturb the pond bottom and the creatures that live there.

For these reasons, I recommend growing water plants, particularly compatible exotics, in pots and changing their pots every year. Each spring, just as they break dormancy, remove the lilies from the pond, dump out the old soil, cut off the old parts of the rhizome, and repot them as you would any sort of potted plant, with new clay soil and a special fertilizer. Water irises should be divided and repotted after they have bloomed and before they have developed new growth and new roots to match.

Any plant grown in a pot in a water garden will have to be repotted periodically, because saturated soils in the pots lose their nutrients over time and have to be renewed. To renew the soil in the pots, bring in soil with a large component of clay, if your garden does not already have this. If you do have clay in your soil, look on it as a blessing, because clay soils hold water better than amended, sandy, or loamy soils.

Repotting with fresh soil temporarily replaces depleted oxygen and replenishes other nutrients such as iron that have been exhausted or chemically changed by yearlong submersion. It also benefits plants by raising the soil pH. I keep a special pile of heavy clay garden soil for water plants. Unlike the acidic soil in the terrestrial garden, this soil is close to neutral. When it goes into the container, its pH is 7.2. After a year's immersion, its pH is 6.8.

At repotting, you might add some fertilizer to a lily pot. (I have not found it necessary to fertilize the water irises.) One fertilizer especially made for water lilies has an analysis of 20-10-5, which means it is 20 percent nitrogen, 10 percent phosphorous, and 5 percent potassium. It also contains small amounts of calcium, sulfur, and iron.

Whenever I repot the lilies, I'm surprised at how vigorous their roots can be. Every year the rhizomes have grown the length of the pot (eighteen inches), and the root ball has completely filled it. The soil almost seems to have disappeared, except for a thin layer of sand at the bottom of the pot.

The Result

It has been fascinating to understand the underwater ecosystem. Now we know why, as we have interfered less, natural processes maintain its health without our involvement, just as natural wetlands have done over the millennia. We began as water gardeners, but we are now stewards of a backyard wetlands habitat. Because it's a manmade wetland habitat, we do watch it. We intervene when the pump quits or when plants need repotting or when one species threatens to take over, but for the most part we leave it alone.

How to Build a Bog Garden

A bog garden can be any size or shape that suits your available space. The basic components, as you can see below, are the same: damp (not wet) soil and plants that like to grow in damp or wet soils. The shape of the cross section is the same, no matter what the size. The

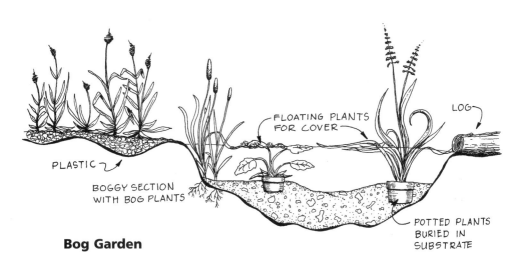

Bog Garden

You can make your bog garden any size and put the plants into pots or directly into the soil or both.

illustration shows a layer of water, similar to a shallow pond, but a bog garden might also have no standing water. A bog garden is a shallow depression in the ground where the soil is always wet. You can pot plants or not, as you choose, but keep in mind that the same possibility exists as in a pond garden of having them overrun the available space.

A natural bog is wetland filled or partially filled with decayed plants, in which the amount of water flowing in is greater than the amount of water flowing out. In some parts of the world, notably Canada, bogs are "peatlands," places where mosses have covered or filled an open area. The sphagnum peat moss so loved by gardeners for hanging baskets and as soil amendments comes from these places. These bogs are quite acidic.

In nature, a boggy place lies close enough to the water table that plants can always have damp roots. Plants that like bogs are the ones gardeners refer to as liking "wet feet." Even in the desert Southwest, bogs occur. They may be caused by seepage from a spring or by water remaining in clay soils. In some areas bogs dry out in the summer; in these places, the animals have adapted to periods of wet and dry. Bog plants can often take some drying, so it may not be critical to keep them wet all year-round. It will depend on what plants you choose. Native bog plants in this area are accustomed to the annual drought, when they become dormant. During the rainy season, they come back, just as the more common perennials do.

To build a bog garden, follow these steps:

1. Dig a shallow depression in the ground. This depression should be no more than a foot deep at the center. The profile of the bog should be dish-shaped, with gradually sloping sides to allow small animals to crawl or hop in and out easily.

2. Put used carpet or a thick layer of builder's sand at the bottom of the hole. This cushions the plastic if you have to walk on it to tend to the plants or if you want to scoop out soil later for testing.

3. Place a sheet of thick plastic or rubber similar in weight to 32 mil PVC liner over the ground so that it extends at least one foot

beyond the sides of the hole. To figure out how much liner you need, add the length of the hole to the depth multiplied by two. Then add that number to the width of the hole to the depth multiplied by two. For example, to figure the amount of liner for a hole approximately 3' wide by 5' long and 1' deep, add 3' + 2' for a width of 5'. Then add 5' + 2' for a length of 7'. This size bog will require a liner 5' by 7'.

4. Put a couple of inches of small gravel, pea gravel, or small stones in the bottom of the hole.

5. If you wish, you can add some organic matter or you can wait for the bog to fill naturally with leaves and other matter. Possible additions include peat moss or leaves from your compost pile. Remember that you want the bog to be as natural as possible, including the natural pH. Bogs tend to be more acidic than neutral, but this depends on the location of the bog. As you fill the hole, you will notice that the plastic wrinkles around the edges and slides toward the bog. Don't worry about this; it's not a problem unless the plastic is too small and the water leaks out around the edges.

6. When the hole is approximately half full of soil, put in the plants. Taller plants and those that can take seasonal drying should go toward the outer edges. Plants that can tolerate standing water all year should go in the middle.

7. Add enough water to weight the soil down around the plants. Continue to add water and soil alternately until the plants' root balls are covered. The water will ensure that there are no air spaces among the roots.

8. Weight the outer edges of the plastic with stones to prevent it from slipping into the bog. (The illustration shows a log weighting down the plastic.)

9. Cut holes in the plastic nearest to the bog and put in plants to make the edges of the bog natural and give land cover to small

Plate 8. Snakes have their place in the ecosystem, too, even in our backyards.

Plate 9. Black wild sunflower seeds attract a variety of small birds at this vertical feeder.

Plate 10. These doves enjoy their ground-feeder arrangement.

Plate 11. A swallowtail butterfly feasts on pansy nectar.

animals. These plants should be those that grow at the edges of natural bogs.

10. Cover the exposed plastic with soil.

To keep the bog constantly moist, you can make it part of the wetland by circulating the pond water into it to be filtered. You can also use your garden hose, either with a small fountain arrangement, or you can water the bog when it shows signs of needing water. You can also put a soaker hose in the bottom of the bog before you fill it with soil and plants.

How to Build a Backyard Wetland

Wetlands in nature are typically arranged in rings, with the deeper water at the center. As the land rises from the center, it becomes drier, and the ecology changes. Plant communities that are able to grow in similar conditions develop.

Aquatic plants—those that can grow in deeper water—are at the center. These are able to live with their roots and shoots in the water. Water lilies grow with only the surface of their broad leaves and the flowers at the surface. Some plants, such as pondweed (*Potamogeton* spp.), are totally submerged and never rise above the surface at all. They carry on all the plant processes, like photosynthesis, underwater.

In the next ring live the emergent plants, those that can live with their roots in water, but their shoots emerge from the water. This ring includes cattails, pickerel rush, arrowheads, bulrushes, grasses and sedges, and lots of wildflowers.

In general, the higher the ground occupied by the plant, the more drying it can tolerate. Some of these plants are able to grow closer to the deep water than others, because they can tolerate "wet feet" longer. Some plants need periods of drying along with periods of wet.

Some wetlands have more acidic conditions than others because they are more affected by larger amounts of rain. A wetland in western Washington and Oregon, for example, with its annual precipitation of thirty-five inches per year, is more acidic than a wetland in eastern Washington and Oregon that only gets nine inches per year. In wetlands around the Great Salt Lake or in other desert areas that dry up completely every year, more salt will remain from evaporation.

If you pay attention to some of these conditions and buy plants close to home, you will have more success with your backyard wetland habitat. It can be any size, from thousands of gallons to the single small pond the size of a bathtub. It can be any shape, as long as it's not rectangular. As I mentioned in the design chapter, there are no straight lines in nature.

A backyard wetland is an underwater ecosystem that doesn't need you to engage in a constant battle against algae and scum. You put in the ingredients and keep the water in constant circulation, so it has plenty of oxygen. Getting oxygen into the water by stirring it up is called *aeration.* It happens when rain falls into a pond, too. Submerged plants also put oxygen into the water; that's called *oxygenation.* Natural filtration and a balance of plants with fish and light with shadow will keep the pond clean and the water aerated for a healthy underwater environment. A healthy backyard wetland is very little work; once it gets going, it stays fresh.

The recipe for building a pond to use as a backyard wetland is much like that for building a bog garden, only bigger. After deciding where you want to put your pond, begin by digging the hole (or holes if you intend to recirculate water between two or more ponds). Then, follow these instructions.

Plan Your Wetland Garden

Decide how many ponds you want to handle. If you have room or funds for only one pond, decide how you will keep the water fresh and recirculate it. A fountain with a pump in the middle of the pond is one way; the splashing makes a pleasant, cooling sound on a hot day and aerates the water at the same time.

The next larger arrangement would be a system with one pond and one holding tub or tank. A pump in the larger pond could pump water into the tank from which it could flow down a waterfall. With this arrangement, also, the splashing is pleasant and the water is aerated.

Alternatively, you might place a pump outside the pond, above the ground and camouflage it with stones and plants. It could pump water up and over the waterfall there, too. The alternatives are limited only by your imagination.

Plan how you will replenish the water lost to evaporation. The simplest means is by a hose. We have an underground pipe with a valve that trickles in fresh water during the annual drought and is turned off during the rainy season (see diagram on page 121).

Some counties or municipalities have ordinances about "attractive nuisances," so learn what the laws are in your area and plan for safety measures. Be sure to arrange a fence of some sort around your wetland garden so small children can't fall in and drown.

You can roughly figure how many gallons each pond holds with these formulas for different shapes—rectangular, circular, or oval. Each formula assumes for simplicity's sake a one-foot depth. Sloping sides will reduce the number of gallons by approximately a third to a quarter.

For a basically rectangular or square pond (or two), follow this formula:

Length x Height x Depth x 7.5 gal/cubic foot

10' x 10' x 1' x 7.5 = 750 gallons

For a circular pond, follow this formula:

(Radius squared) x Depth x Pi x 7.5 gal/cubic foot

(5' x 5') x 1' x 3.14 x 7.5 = 589 gallons

For a 15' x 10' x 1'-deep oval pond, follow this formula:

(½ major axis) x (½ minor axis) x depth x Pi x 7.5 gal/cubic foot.

7.5' x 5' x 1' x 3.14 x 7.5 = 883 gallons

Assemble the Hardware

You will need the following hardware to make the ponds work:

- A thick PVC plastic or rubber liner for each pond. When exposed to UV rays, liners disintegrate over time, and black absorbs more rays than green. However, with the method we've developed, covering all of the liner, very little of it should be exposed to UV rays. The liner should be the length of the hole plus twice the depth added to the width of the hole plus twice the depth. For example, a hole approximately twelve feet by nine feet by two feet deep will require a liner sixteen feet by thirteen feet.

We do not recommend concrete for lining the pond. Concrete has too many drawbacks. It is very heavy to work with, and once it is installed, it has to cure for six to ten months to be sure the toxins are out, before you can safely attract animals to your pond or stock it with fish. In winter where the ground freezes and heaves, then thaws and contracts, concrete is subject to cracking. Once it cracks, you can repair it with a sealer, but the sealer then has to cure for several months in order to get the toxins out.

- A submersible pump, if you intend to put it in the pond. The pump should be capable of moving half the water each hour. For example, in our 4,000-gallon system, the pump moves 2,000 gallons of water per hour.

- PVC pipe. We don't recommend any pipe smaller than ¾", or the pump won't move enough water to aerate the pond properly. We use a 1" pipe. We found that, by using the larger size pipe, we moved much more water in an hour than we had with the smaller size and increased the oxygen supply in the water.

- Materials for assembling the pump and pipes: PVC tape, elbow joints, glue, tubing, etc.

- Fountains, bubblers, and other devices you want for aerating the water.

- Pots for plants, unless you plant them directly in the pond bottom.

- Stones for holding the liner in place. You will need enough stones to lay side by side along the perimeter of the pond. Each stone should weigh about five pounds.

- High rubber boots. You may be getting into the water to make adjustments as the pond fills.

Dig the Hole

All of the water garden books that I've looked at tell you to lay out the shape of your pond with a garden hose on the ground, dig the hole, put in the liner, and hold the liner in place with a rim of large stones around the edge. These stones generally overhang the water by a half inch or more. This method leaves the pond looking like a swimming pool. There are no rings shading from aquatic to wet woods or prairies for different plant communities, and the danger is real for small creatures to jump in and be unable to climb out again over the overhanging edging stones. With the method we have devised, the pond will look completely natural, as if it had been on your property all the time.

During the planning phase, you decided where you want the wetland and how much water you want it to circulate. Now you can start digging.

How large a hole you want depends on the space you have available. How deep a hole depends on your climate. If you live where winters are fierce, in Minnesota or Wyoming, dig the hole deep enough so that fish and other animals can survive the winter without being frozen. In very cold winters this might be about five feet deep at the center.

The greatest danger to fish and other aquatic animals is not from freezing, usually, but from smothering. Fish and other animals take in oxygen and give off carbon dioxide; plants take in carbon dioxide and give off oxygen. In northern winters, water plants are dormant while fish are hibernating, so the only way oxygen enters the water is through some exchange of oxygen molecules with the air. This exchange is helped along by breaking the surface of the water with rainfall, or by air bubblers and fountains. When water is open, carbon dioxide can escape from the pond into the atmosphere.

When ice completely covers the pond for days or weeks at a time, carbon dioxide builds up inside the water and cannot escape. Aquatic animals die from lack of oxygen, perhaps more often than from freezing. You can prevent this from happening with a water heater that you can purchase from a local or mail order supplier or by recalling a simple fact of physics: Moving water does not freeze. Having said that, I must admit that I've seen frozen waterfalls in the Rockies and in the Cascades. If you live where winters are that severe, you might want to consider a heater.

The least satisfactory solution is to break the ice: The booming sound of a sledge hammer or other tool hitting the ice can shock the peacefully hibernating creatures under water. If you must break the ice, do so twice daily at the same spot, to minimize the noise underwater.

As you dig the hole for your pond, plan to dig a level shelf all around the circumference, about six inches to a foot below the rim. The stones go on this ledge. Keep the shelf as level as you can all the way around.

Slope the sides down from the top to the bottom. Don't forget, you want small creatures to be able to get in and out again safely (see the photo below).

While you're at it, carve a route for yourself to get into and out of the pond. Even though it's to be as natural as possible, you may have to get in to repot water lilies and fix the pump. Our pump casing periodically has to be freed of silt and small debris to prevent it from overheating.

Make the interior of the hole as smooth as you can. Remove sharp rocks and sticks and roots that may poke through the liner.

Step 1: Dig the bare hole.

Step 2: Line the shelf with stones.

Put in the Edging Stones

When the hole is as large as you want it and the shelf is as level as you can make it, lay in the stones, end to end, around the entire circumference of the pond (see the photo on this page).

Put in the Liner

When the hole is finished, put in a padding of newspaper or old carpet as a precaution against protruding sharp rocks and sticks. The photo on the next page shows the length of old carpet that we used to underlay the plastic liner.

After you have padded the hole, lay out the liner so that it falls as evenly as possible all around the hole.

Fit the liner to the hole. Get into the hole and walk around on the liner to make sure it's settled into the nooks and crannies. We have a waterfall at one end of the lower pond; you may have a similar feature. The hole is sort of rounded, and the liner is flat, so it will want to fold in places. That's okay. Let it fold where it wants to. The only precaution to take is to ensure that water doesn't leak out.

When the liner is fitted to the bottom and sides of the hole, tuck it over the stones (see the photo on the top of page 141). Make sure the

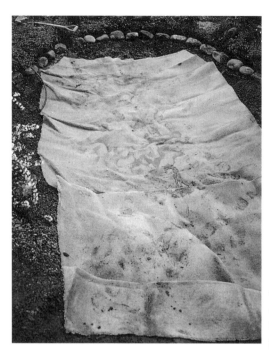

Step 3: Lay an old carpet, such as this, or newspapers, into the hole to provide protection for the plastic liner.

liner is snugly tucked in and be prepared, as you fill the hole with water, to get in and make adjustments.

Put in the Starter Material

You may want to begin immediately to develop a natural bottom to your pond. If so, I'd recommend putting down a layer of crushed rock for two reasons: First, it will give the nitrifying bacteria a place to live. Second, it will help to shield the liner from potentially damaging UV rays of the sun.

If possible, do not use pea gravel, which is smooth. Smooth rock will slip more than crushed rock, which clings better against itself. Line the entire pond with approximately two inches of this rock. If you have sloped the sides, you won't have much trouble with the rock's tendency to obey gravity and slide to the bottom of the pond. If it does over time, you can rake it up again.

We line the bottom and sides as evenly as possible, as shown in the photo on the bottom of page 141. If the sides slope gently, all of the rock won't slide down into the bottom. Be prepared during the seasons, though, to find that you have to rake some rock upward. Animals will

Step 4: With the help of friends, lay in the liner, wrapping it around the stones.

Step 5: Line the pond with crushed stones or some other natural substance to cover the liner.

shove some of it down as they drink, and rain will wash some of it down as well.

Put in the Pump

Now install the pump and other hardware, including pipes, according to your plan and the instructions on the box. Your local hardware store will also help you with instructions on installing PVC pipe. We put our pump into a brown plastic dishpan filled with small gravel. This arrangement helps filter out debris before it can clog the pump, although periodically we turn off the pump and clean out the gravel and the pump's guard. The brown color of the dishpan is nearly invisible when we look into the pond (see the photo below).

We keep our pump running all year-round to aerate the water. Our winters, however, are mild in comparison to those in Montana or Minnesota. In our most severe winter, we will have freezing temperatures (as low as fifteen or twenty degrees) for about a month.

If you intend to have a fountain, or other water-circulating device, install it now.

You can place your ponds at different heights. The following table

Step 6: Place the plants in the hole and gradually fill it with water.

explains how many gallons per hour a small pump will circulate through 1-inch and ¾-inch pipes at various heights.

Discharge Height

Discharge Height	One ft	Three ft	Five ft	Ten ft	Fifteen ft	Twenty ft
1" pipe	1,224	1,200	1,140	960	780	480
¾" pipe	1,040	1,020	969	816	663	408

If you're concerned about the cost of running your pump all year-round, you might use this formula to figure it out:

Watts x Hours x Cents/KwHr x 365 days/year (KwHr is Kilowatt Hour)

For example:

380 x 24 x $.05 = $.46 per day x 365 = $166.44 per year.

Install the Subsidiary Pond

In your case, there may be no subsidiary pond, depending on the space you have and how ambitious you feel. But there should be a biological filtering device or a place for the water to go when you are recirculating it. This may be an above-ground filter, a smaller pond (our solution), or half of a whiskey barrel. In any event, water is pumped out of your main pond to the secondary pond or catch basin and through the above-ground filter, and circulates back into the main pond. The subsidiary pond does not have to be large, as you can see from the photo of our upper pond in winter (see Plate 12, following page 164 *180*).

Where winters are severe, we wouldn't recommend any sort of above-ground mechanism, because it will freeze too readily unless it is well banked with soil and rocks.

No matter what size or arrangement you select, the principles are the same. Water gardening suppliers can help you with pumps and other devices, such as filters.

Put in the Plants

Now, for gardeners, comes the fun part. You can put in your plants. We begin with plants in pots because, at first, unless you add soil to the pond, they will have nothing to grow in.

We start at the bottom of the pond with the plantings, and put in the aquatic plants, both the submerged grasses and water lilies, first (see the photo on page 142). These go in the deepest part of the pond.

Next, we place the emergent plants, those that like to grow in water but want to have their stems and leaves above the surface. These we place at the edges, just down from where the waterline will be. With seasonal fluctuations in the level of the pond (unless you have a continuous trickle of water coming into it), these plants may be more or less in the water. Plant them where their roots will stay covered by water.

At the end of this chapter you will find tables of plants that are suitable for the different rings of the wetland garden.

Fill the Pond

Now begin to fill the pond with water. Fill slowly. When it is about one-third full, turn on the pump to test your installation. As the pond fills, the weight of the water will drag on the liner. Be prepared to shut the water off and make adjustments. Over the next few days, check the ponds daily to be sure everything is running well.

After about a week, or when you're sure everything is in order, stock the pond with fish. Other animals will find your pond; do not bring in frogs or other amphibians.

Plants for Wetlands

Construction is the necessary basis of a successful wetland habitat or a water garden. For me, though, planting is the fun part. I get a vision, sometimes no more than a vague inkling, of what the garden should look like and work toward it over time. As I've learned more, I've let changes happen, so what started as a water garden is being transformed slowly into a wetland habitat.

Some plantings have occurred by accident, or by the contribution of the animals, as in the terrestrial garden. Some native sedges have appeared slightly above the waterline. The dagger-leaf rushes have settled in above the Louisiana irises that grow at the water's edge. These plants attracted frogs and other amphibians that hibernate in mud over the winter.

Further away, our native sword ferns, lady ferns, and bracken ferns grow where their roots are damp for ten months of the year and totally dry during the other two months. I've also planted some other nonnative ferns for contrast with the sword ferns' leaves.

It's a beautiful picture to see the tall bracken fern arching over the clumps of sword fern. The greens and the structures of their fronds contrast with each other. Other ferns you can get include the royal fern, ostrich fern, and cinnamon fern. But watch out, these are all big plants. Some of the sword ferns in our garden have formed clumps four feet tall and ten feet in diameter.

Ferns also give amphibians a place to hide, which is why we very seldom cut back the old fronds to "tidy up" the sword ferns. We leave the bracken ferns up through the autumn, too. They turn yellow and then golden tan, in an effective color contrast with the evergreen sword ferns.

There are also many native wildflowers that grow in wet or boggy conditions. Perhaps no place in the country has such a wealth of native wildflowers for damp soils as the prairies. When I think of a wetland meadow, I see a carpet of colors. Imagine a warm sunny day, with a cooling breeze drifting among blue, yellow, red, and pink blossoms nodding on swaying green stems, with hummingbirds, butterflies, and bees adding their own colors in motion. We humans admire such a picture for its beauty, but for the creatures living among these flowers, they are sources of nectar, pollen, and seeds—vital nutrients.

Of course, if you have lots of space and you want a conversation piece, you could put in *Gunnera manicotta*, the giant of all water or bog plants. Its leaves are typically about six feet long, and it can grow to twelve to eighteen feet, given enough space and time. I've seen examples of this plant in England, at the Royal Horticultural Gardens at Wisley, for example, that looked like small islands in a lake.

There are many good to excellent sources of information regarding wetland plants. For the tables, I've relied on the Web pages of the cooperative extension services in Michigan, North Carolina, Ohio, and Washington; the Northern Prairie Wildlife Research Center; the Lady Bird Johnson Wildflower Center (formerly the National Wildflower Research Center) in Austin, Texas; the National Wildlife Federation; and the EPA.

Among books, the best I've seen yet for wetlands is the *Audubon Society Nature Guides to Wetlands.* Other good sources include the *Manual of Woody Landscape Plants* by Michael A. Dirr; *Wetland Plants of Oregon & Washington* by B. Jennifer Guard; and *Gardening with Native Plants of the Pacific Northwest* by Arthur R. Kruckeberg.

The tables that follow represent very small samplings of the rich array of aquatic plants, ferns, grasses and sedges, flowers, rushes, shrubs, and trees for a variety of wetland conditions. Aquatic plants live mostly or completely underwater, with just their leaves or flowers above the surface. They have adapted to wet or damp soils by developing air spaces in their roots and stems for storing oxygen. Because they all live completely or partially submerged, I haven't listed the tolerance level.

For the other tables, I've given the common name, the Latin name, the range the plant may naturally be found in, and its tolerance to water in the soil. The common name is the English name by which we usually know a plant. The Latin name is more precise and a nursery will help you identify the right plant for your garden. The range is general and divided into broad sections of the contiguous United States. The eastern United States includes all states east of the Mississippi River. Northeast includes New England and the states east of the Mississippi River south to the old Mason-Dixon line. The Southeast includes all of the states south of that line and east of the Mississippi. The South includes all of the southern states from Atlantic to Pacific, while the Southwest includes all of the southern states west of the Mississippi, and Southern California. (Being primarily a desert area, the Southwest is not well represented in these wetland tables.) The Midwest encompasses all the states west of the Mississippi River to the Rocky Mountains. The West includes the Rocky Mountain states to the Pacific Ocean, and the Pacific Northwest takes in Oregon, Washington, Idaho, and western Montana.

The tolerance level is an indication of how much moisture the plant will accept or thrive in. Tolerance is based loosely on the ring the plant is commonly found in. Swamps, marshes, and bogs refer to areas with more to less water. The usual definition (so far as water level is concerned) places swamps at the second ring with more water, then marshes, with less water, and bogs at the outer ring with waterlogged soil. Wet or moist woods and soils refer in a vague sort of way to more or less water in the soil.

As always, do please check with your local cooperative extension service to be sure none of these plants are noxious weeds in your area. Even if you don't find a plant there, ask your local native plant society about plants suitable for wetlands, and avoid if at all possible planting anything that might alter the ecology of the natural areas. After all, we're trying to provide a habitat for wildlife; it's counterproductive to contribute to the destruction of natural areas that support the very wildlife we're trying to help.

Aquatic Plants

Common Name	Latin Name	Range
American lotus	*Nelumbo lutea*	Mississippi basin
buttercup	*Ranunculus* spp.	nationwide...
yellow buttercup	*R. flabellaris*	except Southeast
white buttercup	*R. longirostris*	except Southeast
duckweed	*Lemna* spp.	nationwide
pondweed	*Potamogeton* spp.	nationwide
yellow pond lily	*Nuphar variegatum*	Northeast, Midwest
yellow water lily	*Nymphaea mexicana*	South
yellow water lily	*Nuphar lutea* ssp. *polysepala*	Northwest

Ferns

Common Name	Latin Name	Range	Tolerance
berry bladderfern	*Cystopteris bulbifera*	Northeast	bogs
deer fern	*Blechnum spicant*	Pacific Northwest	moist woods
lady fern	*Athyrium filix-femina*	Pacific Northwest, California	moist woods
maidenhair fern	*Adiantum pedatum*	Pacific Northwest	moist soils
marsh fern	*Thelypteris* spp.	East, Midwest	bogs
royal fern	*Osmunda regalis*	Midwest, Pacific Northwest	bogs
sword fern	*Polystichum munitum*	Pacific Northwest, California	moist woods

Grasses and Sedges

Common Name	Latin Name	Range	Tolerance
arrowhead	*Sagittaria latifolia*	nationwide	swamps
cattail	*Typha* spp.	nationwide	swamps, bogs
cotton grass	*Eriophorum polystachion*	nationwide, except West Coast	swamps, bogs
pickerelweed	*Pontederia cordata*	East, Midwest	marshes
sedge	*Carex* spp.	nationwide	wet soils
cordgrass	*Spartina* spp.	West, Midwest	wet soils
manna grass	*Glyceria* spp.	West, Midwest	marshes
wool grass	*Scirpus* spp.	nationwide	swamps

Flowers and Rushes

Common Name	Latin Name	Range	Tolerance
arrow arum	*Peltandra virginica*	East	swamps, bogs
aster	*Aster* spp.	nationwide	wet soils
bog arum	*Calla palustris*	East	wet soils
blue flag	*Iris versicolor*	Northeast, northern Midwest	swamps
horsetail	*Equisetum* spp.	nationwide	bogs, wet soils
horned bladder-wort (carnivorous)	*Utricularia cornuta*	East, Midwest	bogs, wet soils
jack-in-the-pulpit	*Arisaema triphyllum*	East	wet woods, swamps
Japanese water iris	*Iris ensata*	nonnative	wet soils
lady's slipper orchid	*Cypripedium reginae*	Northeast, northern plains	swamps, wet woods
Louisiana iris	*Iris louisianna*	Southeast	swamps
marsh marigold, cowslip	*Caltha* spp.	nationwide	wet soils, swamps
marsh milkweed	*Asclepias* spp.	nationwide	marshes, bogs
mountain bluebell (lungwort)	*Mertensia ciliata*	interior West	wet soils
pitcher plant	*Sarracenia minor*	Southeast	marshes, bogs
red iris	*Iris fulva*	Southeast	swamps
rose mallow	*Hibiscus moscheutos*	East	marshes
rush	*Juncus* spp.	nationwide	marshes, swamps
Siberian iris	*Iris sibirica*	nonnative	wet soils
skunk cabbage	*Symplocarpus foetidus*	Northeast	marshes, bogs, wet woods
southern blue flag	*Iris virginica*	Southeast	swamps
spike rush	*Eleocharis* spp.	nationwide	swamps
sweet flag	*Acorus calamus*	nationwide	swamps

Shrubs for Wetlands

Common Name	Latin Name	Range	Tolerance
inkberry	*Ilex glabra*	East	moist soils
winterberry	*Ilex verticillata*	East	marshes
bunchberry	*Cornus canadensis*	nationwide, except the South	wet woods
witch hazel	*Hamamelis virginiana*	East, except the Deep South	moist soils
red osier dogwood	*Cornus* spp.	nationwide	bogs
elderberry	*Sambucus* spp.	East, western Washington	wet woods
western azalea	*Rhododendron occidentale*	Pacific Northwest	moist soils
Pacific rhododendron	*Rhododendron macrophyllum*	North Pacific Coast	moist soils
great laurel	*Rhododendron maximum*	East, South	moist soils
honeysuckle	*Lonicera involucrata*	North	moist soils
trumpet honeysuckle	*L. sempervirens*	East	moist soils
red osier dogwood	*Cornus sericea (C. stolonifera)*	North, coast to coast	moist soils
serviceberry	*Amelanchier alnifolia*	nationwide except Southeast	moist soils
snowberry	*Symphocarpos* spp.	North	moist soils
swamp honeysuckle	*Rhododendron viscosum*	East	swamps
water tupelo	*Nyssa aquatica*	South	swamps
willow	*Salix* spp.	nationwide	wet soils
pussy willow	*S. discolor*	Northeast	wet soils
black willow	*S. nigra*	Midwest	wet soils
peachleaf willow	*S. amygdaloides*	Midwest	wet soils
hoary willow	*S. candida*	Midwest	wet soils
sandbar willow	*S. exigua*	Midwest	wet soils

Trees for Wet or Damp Woods

Common Name	Latin Name	Range	Tolerance
alder	*Alnus* spp.	Northeast	moist soils
red alder	*A. rubra*	Pacific Northwest coast	moist soils
mountain alder	*A. tenuifolia*	Rocky Mountains	moist soils
ash	*Fraxinus* spp.	nationwide	moist soils
green ash	*F. pennsylvanica*	East, Midwest	moist soils
Oregon ash	*F. latifolia*	Pacific Northwest coast	moist soils
bald cypress	*Taxodium distichum*	Southeast	swampy soils
birch	*Betula* spp.	nationwide	moist soils
river birch	*B. nigra*	Southeast	moist soils
cottonwood	*Populus* spp.	nationwide	wet or moist
eastern cottonwood	*P. deltoides*	Midwest, Southeast	wet soils
black cottonwood	*P. balsamifera*	Pacific Northwest coast	wet soils
honey locust	*Gleditsia triacanthos*	East	moist soils
maple	*Acer* spp.	nationwide	wet/damp soils
silver maple	*A. saccharinum*	East	wet soils
bigleaf maple	*A. macrophyllum*	Pacific Northwest coast	damp soils
red maple	*A. rubrum*	East	wet soils
Rocky Mountain maple	*A. tenuifolia*	Rocky Mountains	damp soils
"false" cedars	*Thuja* spp.	nationwide	damp soils
western red cedar	*T. plicata*	Pacific Northwest coast	damp soils
northern white cedar	*T. occidentalis*	New England and Great Lakes	damp soils
willow	*Salix* spp.	nationwide	wet soils

When you have finished building and planting your wetland habitat, congratulate yourself. You will have done something good for the small creatures who will be invited to your wildlife sanctuary garden. As a bonus, you will have something beautiful to enjoy. We hope you will enjoy your water garden as much as we have enjoyed ours (see Plate 13, following page 164).

180

Chapter 6

Benign Pest Control

Every region of the country has pests that gardeners refer to with colorful, descriptive language. The concept of a pest in a wildlife sanctuary garden is not an easy one, nor are the solutions. As with the idea of the wildlife garden itself, ideas about pests vary along a wide spectrum of opinion, from the pure wilderness approach, in which nothing is a pest, to the single species approach, in which birds or butterflies or amphibians are the focus of the garden and all other creatures are pests.

Some creatures have their place in nature but most definitely not in a garden. Among these are the truly dangerous reptiles, such as timber rattlesnakes or cottonmouth water moccasins. These reptiles can, of course, be found even in gardens that don't cater to wildlife. Some insects are intolerable to humans too, the fire ant, for example. Northern gardeners can feel extremely fortunate that these pests are not found in cold climates. Of course, Canadian and Minnesotan gardeners can testify to mosquitoes the size of stealth bombers.

The bane of gardeners on the west slope of the Cascades is the slug, that slimy, voracious consumer of herbaceous plants. Theories abound as to how to destroy these slimy critters: sink small plastic tubs of beer in the ground, pour salt on them, handpick them at dawn on moist

153

mornings. Several commercial remedies exist, but they are toxic to birds and pets. Some years ago there was even a cookbook written about slugs. Naturally, all the recipes were totally inedible. They involved consuming copious amounts of whiskey while cooking.

I have to confess that, although I've never cooked a slug, I used to do battle royal with them. And I freely confess that I lost, as anyone will who tries to fight nature. Now, except for two hostas, which are irresistible to me and (alas) to slugs, I plant what slugs don't eat—woody flowering shrubs, columbines, clematis, Japanese anemones, Rodgersia, hellebores, and others. For the hostas, I tolerate some damage that does not imperil the plant.

This approach to gardening is peaceful and much less work. It means, of course, that I can't grow some of my favorites. Delphiniums and cardinal flowers (*Lobelia cardinalis*) are slug food. But since deciding not to plant what slugs eat, I've learned more about plants and have found new favorites—species rhododendrons, azaleas, hardy fuschias, and cyclamen, for example.

I've also discovered that slugs have an important place in the garden. They're part of nature's cleanup crew. One gray, damp June day I was deadheading old flowers off the rhodies when I was alarmed to see that gazillions of slugs covered the leaves. As I stood in shock, wondering how I would ever cope with all this infestation, I realized they weren't eating the leaves. They were eating the spent blossoms that had fallen onto the leaves. I finished deadheading (a form of proactive pruning) and left the slugs to their feast. Within a few days, the beautiful leathery leaves were clean. The garden had taught me another lesson. Even slugs can be a gardener's friend. Picking the blossoms off the rhodies is another job I don't have to do, and slugs also clean up dog poop and other stuff.

What to do about some pests is a matter of personal choice and conscience, and it isn't my place to tell you what to do. As with the whole idea of wildlife gardening, what you do depends on your circumstances and the choices you can make.

The fewer pesticides—herbicides and insecticides—you can get by with, the better for you, your family, and the planet. None is best of all. I call that the first principle of wildlife gardening. The more organic the garden, the more hospitable it will be to wildlife of all sorts and the better luck you will have in getting the balance of nature to work for you. The insecticide that kills mosquitoes may also kill honeybees and butterflies, the spiders that would trap and eat the mosquitoes, and the frogs for whom the mosquitoes are a dietary staple. The herbicide that kills unsightly dandelions may also kill the frog that hops across the dandelion and the bird that grubs about for bugs among its leaves. Dandelions, don't forget, attract butterflies, though they may repel you and your neighbors.

However, some measures may be necessary in your area to protect your investment in your property. While some wildlife gardeners use no insecticides at all, we have an ecologically aware exterminator who sprays every three months around the foundations of our house to prevent carpenter ants. This does kill the spiders that might kill the ants, but we limit the spraying to the building itself and to the foundation. The exterminator does not spray adjacent shrubs and flowers.

The Principles of Benign Pest Control

As we've learned about pest control methods over the years, partly from reading and partly from the garden itself, we've discovered certain principles we go by in controlling pests:

- Tolerate some damage to plants from the pest, if the plant isn't in danger.

- Count on the food chain and natural predators to take care of most pest populations.

- Work with the environment.

- Some pests aren't.

Tolerate Some Damage

Something was eating the snowball shrub. Many of the leaves had curled into tight balls and some sort of chrysalis had formed in the one or two I looked at. My first panicked thought was to spray (old habits die hard), but since the snowball was near the bird feeder, I thought I had better not. I decided to wait and see what happened. About three days later the shrub was alive with birds—chickadees, nuthatches, house finches, sparrows, and juncos. They took care of whatever was infesting the snowball.

Since then, I've trusted the birds to take care of all the bugs in the garden. They've rewarded me with a pest-free garden. Except, of course, for the slugs, which the ducks eat when they visit in the spring.

From this experience arose the second principle.

Count on the Food Chain

Many of the creatures you invite into your domain will dine on each other. Other animals will drop by to take potluck, too, as the heron did with our fish. That's nature.

One summer morning a hawk came to check out the garden as a dinner source. It sat on the fence and thought things over. While it was there, the garden was still as ice. Nothing moved, except leaves in a slight breeze. Not even us. Awestruck, we stood at the kitchen window watching the hawk watch the garden. After some minutes, it flew away. Gradually, tentatively, motion and life returned.

Some people don't want the hawk to get the little birds or the heron to eat their fish. But that's nature at work. It may be the downside of wildlife gardening, but gardeners do best to let it alone.

Slugs eat spent leaves; ducks eat slugs; ladybugs eat aphids; nematodes eat root weevils; and birds eat bugs and their larvae. Some of those larvae might have turned out to be beautiful butterflies, but that's nature's way of taking care of overpopulation. Gradually, through natural selection, the stronger of the species survives, and the species as a whole is better able to withstand external forces that might render it extinct.

If you work with nature instead of against it with chemicals, you will find your invited guests feasting on less welcome inhabitants. The less welcome, though, have to be there for the welcome guests. And even some of the so-called pests—like slugs—have their uses.

That's the upside of wildlife gardening.

In the food chain, nearly everything has its natural predators. Once the chemicals are out of the immediate environment, these natural cycles of predator eating prey take over, and the garden becomes healthier. The difficulty of this approach, of course, is waiting for it to happen and fearing the loss of some favorite plants.

Nearly everything I've learned in gardening has been from experience. I started out gardening with hybrid tea roses. They're extremely susceptible to mildew in our damp climate, and I was always battling rust, black spot, and mildew. I spent a small fortune on systemic pesticides and still got infestations of aphids. (A systemic pesticide is one that you apply to the ground and water, and let the plant absorb through the roots. The plant itself becomes poisonous to pests. Unfortunately, it also becomes poisonous to some beneficial insects. And it doesn't always work.) Then I read something about ladybugs in a garden catalog and ordered some (imagine buying bugs!). In short order I had no more aphids and no more ladybugs, either. They consumed everything they liked that I had to offer and flew off for tastier places.

Back when we thought we had to resort to chemicals, it was usually to treat a plant with some sort of environmental disease, like mildew on roses. The experience with roses has led to the third principle.

Work with the Local Conditions
You can avoid many problems when you select the right plant for the conditions in your garden's microclimate. These include humidity, sunshine, shade, available moisture, and soil. These conditions will affect the health of the plant and determine how much work you have to do. If you work against the environment in which the plant lives, you'll have more work to do and less success.

This is what the roses taught me. Everything was wrong for them: They had too little sun, too much humidity, too much rain, too much shade. Although I didn't test for it, our acid soil was probably the wrong pH.

The more you grow plants suited for the conditions, the more successfully things grow, and the fewer pesticides you will find yourself using. The fewer pesticides you use, the more the natural food chains will render pesticides unnecessary.

From that follows the fourth principle, the definition of a pest.

Some Pests Aren't

When it comes to pests, wildlife gardeners think differently than other gardeners do. Organic gardeners concentrate on the least harmful ways of protecting their food harvests. Most other gardeners look for ways to prevent damage to their plants. They think of pests as creatures that attack their plants: Aphids and slugs come most readily to mind for me. To a vegetable gardener, the cabbage white butterfly larva is to be exterminated, not attracted.

Integrated pest management (IPM) is a pest-control method that offers many nontoxic solutions, with natural, biodegradable pesticide ingredients, but it will resort to chemical pest controls in the long run, after biological and natural controls have failed. In some cases, this may be necessary to save a food crop from devastation by seventeen-year locusts, for example.

For a wildlife gardener, however, any sort of pesticide interferes with the relationship between plant and animal life. A wildlife garden becomes an ecosystem, a naturally functioning interaction between and dependence of plants and animals on each other. For a wildlife gardener, a pest is a plant or an animal that has the potential, given its multiplying into great enough numbers, to damage the ecosystem of our backyard and perhaps the natural areas around us. In this view, a slug is a garden helper and an aphid is butterfly larva food, but the beautiful purple loosestrife is not only a pest, it's a noxious pest.

In nature, every creature has its place in the web of life. In the garden, though, it's sometimes a different matter, depending on the gardener's point of view. Some people dislike squirrels. Other people think they're cute. Some people resent the hawk that dines on smaller birds and on mice, while others are grateful for their presence in controlling the rodent population.

Our approach to squirrels and other, politically incorrect animals such as starlings (one of the aggressive, nonnative birds that are not protected by federal law) is to make no value judgments about them. We may regret that starlings were introduced into this country from Europe, but so far as this garden is concerned, every creature is just being what it is and trying to survive. I recently read in *The Garden*, the journal of the Royal Horticultural Society, that starlings are the only birds capable of drilling into a lawn and grabbing crane fly larvae. We have squirrel guards on the bird feeders, but our backyard feeders, those we can see from the kitchen window, stand among native shrubs such as western red huckleberry and salal and are easily reached from the cascara tree. While there are cleared areas around the feeders, squirrels are super acrobats and can jump from more than ten feet.

We refill the feeders more often than we might if the squirrels weren't around. Periodically we walk out the back door to scare them off, to give the birds more of a chance. Primarily, though, we offer them corn on the cob, a food that most birds don't eat. We might discourage squirrels more actively, but if we did we'd violate the principles of our sanctuary garden.

This is a trade-off, we think. While the location of the bird feeders makes them accessible to squirrels, their location protects them from hawks. Though we're not opposed to hawks, we wouldn't lure the smaller birds to their deaths for them, either.

Noxious Weeds and Pest Plants

Some nonnative plants are so happy in their adopted environment and so vigorous that they threaten their natural surroundings. These plants start out as harmless garden or water garden plants, but they escape from the garden into the natural areas when birds carry seeds and pieces away with them or when blown into natural areas by the wind. These plants then find conditions so much to their liking that they become highly successful, often colonizing natural areas at the expense of native plant species, damaging the native plant colonies and reducing the food supplies for wildlife. In a land overpopulated by nonnative plant species, wildlife may starve. Because of the damage nonnative plants do to natural areas, these plants may win the dubious honor of being recognized as noxious weeds or pest plants.

Noxious weeds are plants that are illegal to grow or import in certain areas, primarily because of the damage they do to a state's economy. Montana, for example, bans certain plants both because of potential damage to agriculture and because they can invade wilderness areas, lakes, and streams and damage the plant communities on which fish and wildlife depend. Destruction of wildlife affects the state's fishing, hunting, and tourism.

One of the most famous examples of a noxious weed is purple loosestrife (*Lythrum salicaria*). It is considered such a danger to wetlands that in Washington State we're advised to bag it securely in plastic and haul it to a landfill.

States with extensive wetlands, including lakes, often ban such plants as Brazilian elodea or anacharis (*Egeria densa*), Eurasian water milfoil (*Myriophyllum spicatum*), parrot feather milfoil (*Myriophyllum aquaticum*), and cabomba (*Cabomba caroliniana*)—a native plant in the southeastern U.S. These plants have been spread widely throughout the U.S. by both the aquarium and the water garden trade.

Akin to noxious weeds are pest plants. These plants pose serious problems in different areas, but the problems are not currently believed to be as serious as with the noxious weeds. Or as was the case with purple loosestrife for a few years, the extent of the damage may not yet be fully understood.

Some plants, however, such as herb Robert or holly, are invasive and can cause damage to Northwest forests. In the South, water hyacinth is banned because it can choke waterways. Recently, yellow flag iris (*Iris pseudacorus*) has appeared on some lists of banned plants for the same reasons.

Gardeners can help everyone else by becoming familiar with which plants are considered noxious weeds. Generally, the noxious weed laws are meant to protect agriculture, but many of the plants on the noxious weed lists also do grave environmental damage. Nearly every state has a list of noxious weeds, with more or fewer plants. Montana, for example, lists fifteen weeds on their statewide noxious weed list: Canada thistle, field bindweed, whitetop, leafy spurge, Russian knapweed, spotted knapweed, diffuse knapweed, Dalmatian toadflax, Saint-John's-wort, sulfur cinquefoil, Dyer's woad, purple loosestrife, yellow star thistle, common crupina, and rush skeleton weed. Many of these and others appear on the other states' lists of noxious weeds, also.

What to Do about Pest Plants

First, we can all help the situation by not planting anything on our states' lists of noxious weeds or pest plants. Your local cooperative extension service can provide a copy of the list, or you can search the Web by going to your favorite search engine and entering the phrase *noxious weeds.*

Second, if you have already planted some that appear on the lists, begin to eradicate them. Go slowly. Some wildlife probably has made it a habitat or depends on it as a food source. Different plants may need different means of disposal. In these parts, Himalayan blackberry only thrives in full sun; if western red cedar is planted to shade it, it will eventually die. Do not use herbicides to get rid of noxious weeds. That's a case of the cure being worse than the disease.

Third, replace the pest plant with a native plant or a harmless non-native.

We may all regret planting ivy as a groundcover or *Buddleia davidii* to attract butterflies. We may all hate the thought of ripping out a favorite plant because it's a noxious weed. But we can learn to love other plants that have a beneficial effect. The first principle of medicine works equally well in wildlife gardening: "First, do no harm."

When Birds Become Pests

The federal government protects all wild birds except for pigeons, starlings, and English (or house) sparrows. By law, when a wild bird becomes a pest, you may not shoot, trap, or poison it. Sometimes, however, birds can engage in activities that drive humans wild. When I was a teenager, I lived down the block from a house whose upper story was riddled with woodpecker holes. This year, a northern flicker has taken to pounding on one of our metal rain gutters.

The flicker is probably signaling that our house is part of its territory. I watched one morning while it faced down a crow. The crow was much the larger bird, perhaps three times the flicker's size. Both birds were interested in the feeder, with its delicious suet. The flicker drummed. The crow yelled back. Neither bird made a move toward the other or toward the feeder. I'd like to think the crow had a healthy respect for the flicker's sharp beak. (After all, if it could drill through the bark of a tree, think what it could do to a crow.) The flicker, on his side, seemed to have no wish to mix it up with a much larger adversary.

After some minutes of this exchange of drumming and yelling, the flicker flew down to the feeder. The crow told him what he thought of that. The flicker screeched back. Soon the crow flew away. The flicker dined on suet.

Our rain gutter was the flicker's means of communicating with the crow. Sometimes it's his way of letting the world know what he wants to say, perhaps to announce his territory or maybe signal his mate. At any rate, he has done no damage and it has never been enough to irritate us.

But if the bird were to set about drumming at 6:30 A.M. on a Saturday, it might be different. In the case of the woodpeckers, I suspect that the house was prone to some sort of insect the woodpeckers were after. The homeowner could have regarded their activity as a danger signal and called in professional help to get rid of the bugs. That's often why a woodpecker will drill holes in wood siding. In that case we can consider the woodpecker a friend who's warning us of a problem.

The Fish and Wildlife Service has some suggestions for preventing irritating drumming. (The URL for this information is www.fws.gov/mbmo/pamphlet/prob.html#3e.)

Leave a dead tree standing for a snag. Or have one brought in and "plant" it. This gives the woodpeckers an alternate site for their drumming.

If a woodpecker drums a hole in your house, find out why. If there are no bugs, you might caulk the space so there's no sound. Put up something to make the drumming site unattractive: pinwheels, flash tape, or wind chimes.

You might also make an alternate drum and put it inside the bird's territory, where it won't be a nuisance to you. The FWS says, "Fasten two overlapping boards, the back board firmly secured and the front (covered with metal sheeting) nailed to it at only one end." You can attach the back board to a fence post or put up a sturdy post and nail it to that.

Another way that birds become pests is by eating foods from our backyards. If you have cherry or apple trees or raspberries, you can protect them from birds by offering alternative foods. Bird netting covering the trees and berry plants will keep the fruit for you, but I think it's as much a nuisance to put on and take off as the birds themselves. We share our fruit with the birds and with the neighbors.

You can also use netting to discourage fish-eating birds from eating your fish. We tried that and found it too difficult to put netting over the shrubs we planted around the ponds. We traded the netting to a water garden supplier for water lilies. Next, we put up a replica of a heron, because herons are territorial. That didn't end the fish predation. The raccoons got them. So we decided to consider herons and raccoons as wildlife instead of pests, and we put in a few feeder goldfish.

Of course, a change in attitude may be the best method of dealing with pests. Changing our attitude has worked wonders. We now have no bird pests. We simply share the fruits of our yard.

Cats

I love cats. (And dogs.) Three of my best friends have been cats. One disappeared when I was a child, but the other two lived to be fifteen and eleven and died painlessly. If I ever get another cat, though, it will be an indoor cat because I've become aware of the damage to wildlife from free-roaming domestic cats.

The National Audubon Society reports: "Scientists estimate that free-roaming cats (owned, stray, and feral) kill hundreds of millions of birds and possibly more than a billion small mammals in the U.S. each year." Further, birds and small mammals comprise perhaps twenty to thirty percent of the cats' prey. In the U.K., cats are thought to kill seventy-eight million birds every year.

These estimates (and others I've read) are so large they're difficult to believe. But even confirmed cat lovers like me have to accept that feral and free-ranging domestic cats take a terrible toll on wildlife.

Karen Miles, who gardens in Illinois, and is a member of the nature.net wildlife gardening forum, told this sad story:

If anyone knows how to control cats, please let me know. I have been creating a backyard that is attractive to rabbits. I like to see the mothers with their babies in the spring. They DO NOT harm anything in my yard as many people have told me. Last spring an entire litter of six was killed by a cat who was just looking for something to do. It certainly wasn't that the cat was looking for food; it didn't eat any of the babies. It just killed them. I walked out into the yard when it was too late. By the way, I have a six-foot redwood privacy fence that the cat got around somehow. If there is a sonic device to keep out cats, wouldn't it also keep out wildlife?

A sonic device to keep out cats might well keep out wildlife. Cats can get over our six-foot fence, too.

I asked members of the Wildlife Garden Forum for their ideas on controlling cats. Not all of their ideas will work all of the time, but these are all good methods that are worth trying. Keep in mind that cats are extremely persistent and are known for never giving up. These are the responses from forum members.

Jennifer in Canada:

I have heard that sprinklers set to a tripping mechanism will do the job to some extent. Actually its not really a sprinkler so much as a nozzle with a jet stream that comes on for about two minutes. I can imagine though that they could easily get out of the way of the water and still present a threat to your backyard birds.

The average house cat catches and kills an annual average of about 150 birds according to studies done in the lower mainland of BC. That statistic does seem high. I have had cats almost all my life, and I certainly don't see that amount of mortality, but I don't spend my days following my cat around my acre either.

Colleen trains her cats:

I have had several cats, and have been successful in training all of them to leave birds alone—both my birds in the house and the wild ones outside. I have been fortunate in getting all but one as a kitten, which helps. If I do find them too interested in the birds I sit them down and have a VERY stern conversation with them. Cats do not like to be held in place, but I did so as gently as possible, looked right into their eyes, and had that stern conversation about not paying any attention to the birds.

Words don't matter—tone of voice does. Sometimes one reminder may be needed—the cat's name in a "we do NOT do that" tone works just fine for me. If I had a cat that was very stubborn in any area, a light spray of water around its head and then that conversation worked wonders, or if it has made a "mistake" once, I rub its nose in it (the dead bird), then go through the same "conversation" procedure.

Denise reports:

Controlling roaming cats is an ongoing problem for those who wish to attract wildlife. What works for one cat may not work on another. Using a sonic pest deterrent worked well for a cat I had chased away for months. Sprinkling black pepper at the point of entry worked for another. Being consistent seems to work the best. Using any suggestion and trying everything will help you get the results you seek. Public awareness of the dangers to their pets' well-being would probably help. Stray or loose animals are often the target of abuse or even torture. And it is not at the hands of wildlife lovers. Allowing a pet to roam loose and become a mouser or kill rats may lead to secondary poisoning. Owning a pet, whether cat or dog, should carry a responsibility of love to protect the animal from danger. The person who said it was like playing roulette was right!

Alan Courtright recommends putting crumpled chicken wire around the feeders or wherever cats can enter the property:

The idea is to put the chicken wire in the area(s) where the cats enter the property, and/or in a peripheral area around the feeder, so the cats can't get close enough to pounce. Doesn't need much elevating: just a half inch or so.

For the sake of our pets and the wildlife they can destroy, the American Bird Conservancy, the American Humane Association, and the Humane Society of the United States have joined together in an educational campaign to encourage people to keep their cats indoors. The program is called "Cats Indoors Campaign." This is not only for the sake of wildlife, but for the cat's protection as well. Keeping a cat indoors protects it from being killed or maimed by cars and attacks from other animals, from being euthanized to control cat overpopulation, and from catching diseases or contracting parasites. An indoor cat is not prey to cruel humans who shoot it, stab it, set it on fire, or sell it to research laboratories. A cat kept indoors cannot be caught for use as "bait" to train fighting dogs, an illegal, underground activity.

If we want our cats to have the "outdoor experience," the Progressive Animal Welfare Society (PAWS) recommends building an outdoor "run" of sturdy poles and chicken wire that keeps the cat in while letting it see out. The top twelve inches of the run's side fence should be built inward at about a forty-five-degree angle, or roofed completely by the same wire. (If you consider chicken wire to be unsightly, you might be able to find a better-looking substitute.)

Talk to your neighbors who have cats. Explain what you're trying to do with the sanctuary garden and ask for their cooperation in controlling their cats and keeping them indoors. Putting a collar with bells on a cat might not save a wild animal's life; the animal doesn't necessarily associate the sound of bells with danger.

But what about the people who consider it the cat's "right" to roam? I tried to set up a dialogue with a cat-owners' group and was told, less than politely, that cats had rights, too, among them the right to exercise their nature outdoors. To cope with this attitude, we can protect our property by fencing it, although cats (like most wild animals), can get over a six-foot fence or squirm through holes. PAWS recommends a further safeguard along the top of the fence. Nail a series of small stakes pointing outward at about a forty-five-degree angle and string chicken wire along them or nail slats to them. (Be sure to keep within the covenants, if any, in your neighborhood.) If you have a wood fence, or if you are concerned about holes in it, you might nail a small-mesh wire fencing, such as chicken wire, at the bottom and on your side of the fence, about a foot wide.

Controlling other people's cats requires some delicacy. If you can't chase a cat away or scare it off with sonic methods or a sprinkler, and you can't be home to watch over your property all the time, or the dog can't live free in the yard because it might harm wildlife, get rid of the cat—humanely. That predator cat may be a nuisance to you, but it may also be a child's beloved kitty-cat.

First, familiarize yourself with the local laws and ordinances regarding the pet owners' rights. Failure to comply could involve you in legal problems and sizable fines.

Second, buy or rent a humane trap and take the cat to an animal shelter. Put up signs round the neighborhood to notify the owners where they can find their pets. If they care about the cat, they'll retrieve it and ensure that doesn't happen again. If the cat comes back, be prepared to do it again until the owner gets the message.

One winter a "marauder cat" took up residence under one of our bird feeders. Throughout many rainy days, it huddled under the ferns, only running out to grab for a bird. We sent Angus out to chase it off time and time again, but whenever the canine cat deterrent came inside, the "marauder cat" was back. It was such a good jumper that it would crouch at the foot of the feeder pole and snatch a bird out of the feeder, more than six feet off the ground.

Then we tried placing holly, rose, and pyracantha branches all over the ground beneath the feeder, but the cat stepped between the branches. If the winter rains didn't stop it, a water sprinkler would have had no effect, either.

When all other measures had failed, we eventually succeeded in trapping it in a humane trap. We took it to a private shelter that guarantees to find a good home for a stray pet, reunite it with its original owner (on condition of spaying or neutering), or keep it the rest of its natural life. In keeping with our local ordinances, we put up signs all over the neighborhood with the cat's description and the shelter's telephone number. The shelter circulated its description to animal control, in case the owners called them. No one claimed it, but we no longer have a problem with that cat.

Mice and Rats

Cats are great deterrents for mice and rats, if only they would confine their efforts to these creatures. European rats live only around people and are notorious for bearing diseases. Even without a cat, you can prevent rats and mice from invading your living space by taking some simple precautions.

If you compost kitchen scraps and grass clippings and leaves for soil amendments, keep the cover on the composter so the rodents can't get into the kitchen waste before it becomes compost.

If you store birdseed in your garage or in your apartment, keep it tightly covered also. The best containers for seed and other animal foods are metal garbage cans with lids. Mice, rats, raccoons, and squirrels can chew through plastic. It's rather disconcerting to scoop up a bowlful of dog food and find a mouse in it, alive or dead.

Preventing Pests

In a wildlife garden, controlling pests means working with the garden's ecosystem. Once it's functioning, a healthy wildlife garden takes care of itself for the most part, with only minimal intervention from the gardener. Pests and diseases may attack plants and animals, but their own good health will enable them to survive.

You will notice when your garden has become an ecosystem because you'll be watching, which is much of the fun for wildlife gardeners. You'll know the ecosystem functions when butterflies flutter among the flowers, when bees and hummingbirds dart from flower to flower, when birds return to the feeders throughout the day. You'll discover a rhythm in the seasons that isn't only falling leaves, rain, snow, or buds and blossoms, but the arrival or departure of familiar guests and visitors and seasonal inhabitants.

The first flowers on the native Indian plum or *Rhododendron dauricum* "Midwinter" tell me winter won't be around much longer. When the mallard pair returns to the ponds, when frogs raise their voices, and the evening grosbeaks arrive—these events tell me it's spring more than the calendar does. We don't have any pests these days. The ecosystem functions to take care of itself and maintain its own health.

A healthy garden ecosystem attracts animals who will establish the predator-prey cycle that controls pests naturally. Healthy birds, especially the much-maligned starling, will feast on insect and larva pests, including the crane flies that so worry my neighbors. Composting leaves and kitchen scraps adds soil amendments and minimizes the need for supplemental fertilizers. In turn, soil amendments loosen the soil and aerate it so beneficial insects and microbes can get oxygen in the soil. Earthworms aerate the soil, and their castings add nutrients.

Everything works together to make a healthier, more beautiful garden. Plants are stronger and more disease-resistant. They also suffer less damage from pests and recover more quickly if they are attacked.

For the most part, the ecosystem of our yard takes care of pests by itself. By the time you read this I shall have demolished the Himalayan blackberry (a pest in western Washington) that has taken root under the ground-cover rose. First, though, I'll have to locate a suit of armor so I can get under the rose without lacerating myself. Then, I'll wait until cold weather, when the rose has shed its leaves and the young of anything living under it (other than the blackberry) has left the nest (if there is one).

That's pest control in our wildlife garden.

The Ultimate Pest Control: Changing Our Attitudes

Ultimately, pest control means changing our attitudes so that nature's way can work. It's hard not to intervene, sometimes. There are massive invasions of deer and rabbits in places, partly because their natural predators have been killed off and because people are sentimental about Bambi and Thumper. Urban sprawl in this area has meant bear and cougar and coyote in people's yards—or is it that we're in the animals' backyards?

Sometimes people can be jealous of the plants in their gardens. But one of the Wildlife Garden Forum members, Bev in Maryland, had a humane approach to dealing with nuisance wildlife that was destroying valuable plantings:

> *We did have a beaver in our creek a few years back—it built a good-sized dam that was seriously backing up the creek! We were delighted! We were not delighted when we realized that its favorite food was the dogwoods and my neighbor's peach trees! Dogwoods are one of Maryland's most beautiful sights in spring. After a little thought we decided to let the beaver alone and my neighbor put wire around his remaining fruit trees. A couple of floods washed away the dam and we haven't seen any beaver signs for a long time.*

They protected the fruit trees and let nature do the other work for them. Like beauty being in the eye of the beholder, maybe the pest is in the attitude. You alone can decide what's a pest in your garden.

Chapter 7

Benefits of a Sanctuary Garden

When you make a sanctuary garden, everyone benefits—you, your family, and your neighbors—human and nonhuman alike. You and your family have a peaceful and harmonious place to relax and play—and learn. Your neighbors will benefit because you won't be adding pollutants or shredding the morning quiet with your lawn mower. You can invite them in to enjoy the garden with you. In our neighborhood, children love to come and help feed the fish. (The six-foot cedar fence keeps out people, especially small people, when we're not home.)

Your children and grandchildren have a constant source of interest, in learning about nature in a microcosm. Many a small child's enduring interest in the biological sciences has been nurtured by watching insects and animals in their own backyards. That very young person who likes crawly things and whose pockets are full of surprises may be another Jane Goodall.

Even adults (like me!) can have the fun of learning new things. Until this garden taught me so, I didn't know about mason bees that build nests out of mud. I didn't know that some bees would tunnel into old tree stumps underground to make their nests. I didn't know that some hornets collected mud to make their nests. It's fun to watch them gather it while I'm doing repair work around the edges of the ponds or restoring the rocks in the stream. No, they haven't stung me yet.

The sanctuary garden teaches us gently about some of life's hard experiences. It does not protect us. There we come to terms with the reality of death. A baby bird, a possum, a raccoon, a snake, a rabbit—finding these animals who have lived their short spans of life teaches us that death is part of life, that it's natural. We all learn about this, gently from nature or by the hard experience of losing a loved one. When I was little, my father left work to conduct a funeral for a turtle. I was the only mourner. His co-workers thought he was nuts, but I have remembered it all my life. When I lost people I knew and loved, I didn't mourn any less, but I was more prepared than I might have been if not for the turtle.

Robert the Bruce (the Scottish noble who unified and became king of Scotland in the twelfth century) isn't the only one ever to watch a spider build its web and marvel that it sustains itself by hanging in midair on invisible threads of steely strength, nor is he the only one ever to draw parallels between the natural world and our own. Despairing of ever succeeding in bringing his vision of a unified Scotland to reality, he lay sleepless one night, watching a spider try to cast a thread over a distant beam. The spider tried seven times before it succeeded. Unlike Robert the Bruce, we may not be inspired to arise and free Scotland, but we can learn about endurance and perseverance in the midst of troubles.

Understanding plant communities reminds us that we all depend on each other, that we do nothing alone. The book you're reading is the product of many hands. Without the help of the people in the acknowledgments it would not be the book it is. Without Bonnie's delightful drawings, or Dick's super photos, or book designer Tasha Hall's choice of typeface and design—without all these people and more, this book would not be. We all live in communities, and we all depend on each other.

I asked the members of the Wildlife Garden Forum on the Internet why they gardened for wildlife. In essence, they said, "For the joy of it." Tresa Newton in Alabama wrote:

Just something about hearing the distinctive sound of humming-birds all about me as I go about my gardening and knowing that at least in my little corner of the world, they have a sanctuary from man's ever-growing need to change habitats to suit their own needs, pleases me.

For someone who doesn't really consider herself a "wildlife gardener," Kim in Florida said:

> *I garden in the middle of a city block, and the wildlife there is just as important to me as the plants. I garden because it provides a profound sense of clarity and connectedness. To listen to anoles rustle through the arrowhead and ferns, and to watch Gulf frittilary caterpillars eat passion vine gives you an unequaled opportunity to see just how precious life really is.*

(I had to e-mail Kim to ask her what an anole is. She explained that it's a type of salamander.)

Alan Courtright gardens on an island in Puget Sound. He wrote that he gardens for the "speeded-up dynamics. A garden/landscape is dynamic, but on a rather long timescale for human eyes. Animals activate it, the way a fast passage livens up a symphony, and makes one feel more alive. Watching an apple ripen or a plant grow and flower isn't all that enlivening."

Many people garden for the release of tension it brings us after the stresses of the workday world, but for wildlife gardeners there's an added dimension. Diane in Pennsylvania explains:

> *I love the sounds of nature and respect the balance it maintains when not disturbed by humans. I love watching the birds and listening to their unique sounds. I get excited when some new creature wanders into my yard or a new plant pops up that I had not planted in my garden. It is always a challenge to try to identify these things.*
>
> *I like the peace it brings after a bad day at work. I just go out and wander around the pond looking for different creatures or filling the bird feeder while the birds sit in the trees and chirp me out for disturbing them (even though I know they appreciate their feeders being filled). I lose all consciousness of what went on at work that day as I*

walk around the garden and inspect the plants for insects or new sprouts. If I still feel any frustration I just yank a few pesky weeds. Creating a wildlife habitat is my way of giving back what we all have taken from nature.

The poet William Wordsworth (who was the guiding voice of this book's garden design recommendations) felt a bond with the landscape of his native Lake District in England. Wildlife gardeners feel a similar bond with their gardens. They value the sense of connectedness with the earth that comes to them there.

Barb in Michigan writes:

I see my garden and myself as a united entity. When I was forced to move into the city for health reasons, the yard was a barren nothing. Not even bees survived here; I had to hand-pollinate. Not quite four years later, the yard has a surround of natives that is gradually attracting some wildlife. Next year I will add a pond. I am collecting casts of wildlife tracks to impress into the cement to leave the feeling larger wildlife is welcome and may have passed this way. By search-ing out species of plants with food and shelter for wildlife, by provid-ing water and loving care, I become part of my garden and it part of me. We are both far more complete.

Kelly in Portland, Oregon, finds a sense of place in her garden that was missing in her life:

When I was a little girl, we moved almost every year. I went to eleven different schools before graduating from high school. My family lived in every major environment in the Northwest: wet, dry, treed, or sagebrushed. I had very little sense of place, I still find it hard to remember street names and such. After all, why keep data in long-term storage that will be dumped in a few months? All I knew upon reaching adulthood was that I wanted to live somewhere green. My husband and I ended up here. . . . Our tiny eden was once Douglas fir forest crossed by a Native American trail to the coast. Then it was cleared for farming and partially orcharded, abandoned, then reforested in young firs by nature, then logged again. When we purchased this lot, there were no plants taller than eight inches except for the few shrubs left around the perimeter and some undesirable (forked or small) firs left variously strewn about the middle. In my naivete, I thought all I would have to do would be to plant lots of rhododendrons and that would be that. But then I spotted my first native plant—the red flowering currant—and my whole reality changed! I bought field guides and attended a few workshops on native plants. I thought I was doing my bit for the environment or being trendy or PC, but what was really happening was that I was learning what belonged here. I watched in absolute awe as nature returned what should be here, what was meant to be here: Iris tenax, Oregon grape, bearberries, hazelnuts, goldenrods, trillium, violets. What I have come to value most is that, in identifying each new plant and creature, I am achieving that sense of place that I have longed for all my life. I know what should be here and what is missing, and as I watch nature do her incredible job of restoration, and add my stumbling attempts to help it along, I feel as if I am starting to belong someplace. For the first time in my life, I feel intimate with my surroundings, I know where next year's lupines will probably bloom, and where I may be able to see a bull snake; I feel at home.

For most of us, the wildlife garden is multidimensional. Of course, it's visually beautiful. Many people tell me their gardens are best in spring, when the flowers are in bloom. I think ours is beautiful at any time of the year. In the spring most flowers are in bloom, but we have sought out flowers that bloom at any time of the year, so summer flowers satisfy our need for bloom—and the bees' needs for nectar—all year-round. In late summer and autumn, blue asters, pink Watson's willow herbs and Japanese anemones, yellow geums and black-eyed Susans attract bees and the native white butterflies. Pink and white hardy cyclamen light up shady corners. I love the play of sunlight glistening on leaves that sparkle as they flutter in the air and give luster to all the different shades.

But in addition to color, wildlife gardeners experience the sounds of the garden. Birds sing, chatter, and scold; as Diane said, "They chirp us out." In the evenings, ducks and jays have a different voice, when they're talking to each other, than we humans usually hear. Their voices, usually limited in our hearing to strident quacks or racks, take on a chattering sound. I hear the ducks' conversations late in the day, as they settle into the neighboring wetland for the night. It sounds very domestic, as if they were talking over the day while getting ready for bed.

In spring, the native frogs establish their territories, call their mates. They talk. They converse. They challenge and croon. During the dry season, they're living on the land, and they're quieter.

The trees give voices to the air, also. In the rainy season, when the storms come in, the conifers set up a roaring that in the small hours makes me think we could just as well live close to the airport. In summer, the quieter breezes have a gentle, leafy rustle about them. The Douglas firs, hemlocks, and western red cedars add their softer bass hum to the bigleaf maples' alto and the soprano shrubs. When you plant in communities, you get a choir.

And always, because we keep it going year-round, the waterfall gurgles.

The wildlife garden is full of motion from all the life in it. It is literally alive. The insects, animals, and we inhabit it and are in motion. I think this sense of being amidst a living entity is what wildlife gardeners feel in their connectedness. I know I do.

In winter, the architecture of the garden shows through. The perennials are dormant; the deciduous trees and shrubs have lost the leaves that glorified autumn. The conifers and broadleaf evergreens—the *Osmanthus delavayi* and rhododendrons—come into their own. The texture of bark shows in still another dimension, that of touch. The twisty shapes of the hinoki cypress contrast with the stiff pines and Engelmann spruce (*Picea englemanii*).

In all this, as Thelma wrote:

> *Why do I do it? I love flowers and I love nature, especially the birds. It is relaxing to just sit and unwind after a day's work, and watch the birds at the feeders and to identify some. I keep my book close by for that purpose. Between nature and my flowers I feel I am keeping God's coloring book going for others to enjoy as they drive by.*

Wildlife gardeners like Thelma share. We share our spaces with wildlife and with our neighbors.

More than one person wrote about a sense of responsibility toward the planet as a satisfaction in wildlife gardening. These wildlife gardeners understand that urban sprawl is devastating the habitats of urban America, so we like the idea of sharing our property with the original residents. It's a matter of stewardship, of giving sanctuary to some other of God's creation.

Jacalyn in upstate New York writes:

Last week I looked out my kitchen window and saw two white-tailed deer eating breakfast in the meadow that I call my backyard, less than twenty feet from my home. Mr. and Mrs. Rabbit also eat weeds and play in the lawn. This summer I have had the joy of watching and hearing catbirds, cardinals, indigo buntings, kingbirds, Baltimore orioles, and many more. In the fall the coyotes will be wandering again, although, hopefully, they will stay out of my driveway. Nature has given me so much that I am trying to do my small part to share what I can and to learn about and contribute to that beauty and not destroy it.

Joseph in western Washington writes:

I am appalled at the loss of habitat in virtually every corner of our great country. Since I can't take large developments and turn them into natural settings, I'm trying to do my small part to encourage wildlife to flourish in my backyard. It's "saving the world one yard at a time."

There's so much to learn from other living things that I never tire of casual observation and the research it spawns. The needs of each plant and animal are specific and what I've come to realize is that these wild things exist as interactive systems, each dependent on something else for its survival. I get satisfaction believing that I can influence (in a positive way) the fitness or survival of some creature that will never be of any economic benefit to me. The reflection that this viewing inspires can calm me after a difficult day or excite me when

I see something new poking around in my backyard. All I need is to see it or hear it feeding, nesting, or hiding in the plants I've set out for it to enjoy.

We all naturally feel a kinship with other creatures. Witness a child fascinated with their first goldfish or hamster or their first wild-caught garter snake or lizard. My backyard has helped to rekindle that innocent curiosity that tends to get shoved aside in our busy adult world.

I take pride in my oddball yard (with no grass). It's nestled amidst a sea of green desert, surrounded by sterile lawns drowning in chemicals. My neighbors are constantly fighting the good fight to keep their lawns alive and looking healthy, never wondering why they won't stay vibrant without expensive intervention. Now, instead of surrendering my leisure time to lawn maintenance, I can do other things that call to me. I can observe more wild things than just crane flies. If more people would think about working with the natural systems that dictate what will grow and what won't, rather than trying to conquer them, we wouldn't see the mountains of chemicals hauled from the garden stores to be dumped into our soil and water.

The effects of what we do in our little plots can be felt far away. I know this because I've seen wildlife "recolonize" parts of my urban yard as a result of what I've planted there. I only wish I had more real estate to play with.

As an Ohio gardener wrote:

I do it because I feel it's my responsibility to do it. I started out just growing flowers. Then I just felt like I could do more . . . not for me, but for nature. I could grow anything, but I have chosen to grow native plants and wildlife friendly plants. The plants either provide nectar, berries, nuts, or shelter. And every day that some little (or large) form of wildlife shows up that wasn't there before, I know that I'm making a difference. I also hope that when others see how beautiful and peaceful my garden is, that maybe they'll be moved to do something, anything, that might make a difference.

Frank Grazynski is not only a wildlife gardener, but chairman of the Trumbull Land Trust in Connecticut. He writes:

I know that the landscaping techniques I employ (or don't employ), the plants I have, and the pond I built all add to the Earth. The habitat is great, not only for wildlife but for my family too: health aspects are number one, with educational opportunities right up there. The one aspect of the habitat that I can attest to is the tranquility I experience in my gardens. I find it too easy to spend countless hours just watching the birds and frogs and becoming one with the Earth. Great for me, but lousy for the household chores and tasks that get pushed aside.

As Frank points out in another part of his note, that's what a sanctuary garden is all about. Some people find it a source of spiritual renewal and healing, so much so that at least two churches, at opposite sides of the continent, have found it natural to reach out to others through wildlife gardening. Earth Ministry, an ecumenical initiative in Seattle, Washington, and the Community Lutheran Church Earthkeeping Ministries in Sterling, Virginia, both interpret stewardship to include "care for the Creation." Both these initiatives encourage groups of people, i.e., congregations, to work together on projects.

In wildlife gardening, people are taking care of the creation—at least those bits of it that they can control. Their efforts often extend beyond the individual to involve the community at large and sometimes other communities as well. Community Lutheran Church (CLC) had several goals for its Hedgerow Habitat Trail project. First was to "restore and enhance wildlife habitat on its own grounds"; second was to "provide education about what can be done to reduce the impact of urban sprawl on natural communities." Spearheaded by Suse Greenberg, the project began in 1994. When fall planting day arrived in November 1995, the effort had spread beyond CLC to its local community and the Urban Family Institute in Washington, D.C.

The finished trail is 1.5 miles long and includes meadow, forest edge, and wetland habitats, among others (see Plate 14, following page 164). It is structured with sitting areas to enable people to pause to watch wildlife or reflect on their own lives. Through working together to plant this and other gardens, members of the congregation became more involved with inner-city gardening efforts in Washington, D.C., specifically the Morton Park Housing community and the Urban Family Institute. From the beginning, CLC was assisted by Craig Tufts of the National Wildlife Federation.

CLC's pastor, Paul D. Opsahl, says of the effort to build the trail:

> *The effect on the congregation has been profound, involving them in reflection not only on the goodness of creation, but also on our own responsibility as people of faith to care for the earth. At the same time, the interest and involvement of the wider community have been very helpful in creating and maintaining the Trail. Earthkeeping interacts with just about every other ministry of our congregation.*

In a pamphlet titled *Beyond Your Backyard: Conserving Wildlife Habitat in Your Community,* the NWF lists several other community groups that are making their communities better places to live, not only for people, but for wildlife as well.

The sense of well-being and benefits of fresh air and exercise that gardeners have noticed throughout human history has led to several initiatives that link wildlife gardening with health. The People-Plant Council (PPC) was formed after a 1990 symposium, "The Role of Horticulture in Human Well-Being and Social Development." Its mission is to "document and communicate the effect that plants have on human well-being and improved life-quality."

In nursing homes, also, wildlife gardening has found a niche. The Eden Alternative began in the early 1990s with the belief of a young doctor named William Thomas that plants and animals promote the welfare of elderly people. It attacks the "three plagues of nursing homes—Loneliness, Helplessness, and Boredom—by offering residents opportunities for companionship, caring for living things, spontaneity, and variety." The Eden Alternative was first applied in the West at Riverview Care Center in Spokane, Washington. First, the staff put plants throughout the facility. After that, they introduced two indoor cats. Next, they established an aviary, and each resident was given a parakeet of his or her

Plate 12. In winter, the upper pond looks like this in the snow.

Plate 13. The lower pond in summer attracts a variety of dragonflies and amphibians.

Plate 14. The Community Lutheran Church Hedgerow Habitat Trail offers spiritual peace to all who visit, human and nonhuman alike.

own. Last to arrive was Sam the dog. Currently, Riverview has Sam, the two cats, and sixty birds. Each resident has his or her own bird, if they want one.

Perhaps eighty percent of the residents are not physically capable of caring for the animals, but they can tell the staff members that a cage needs changing or their bird needs to be fed. Doing that much gives the elderly a sense of control that is usually missing in a nursing home. The animals and plants have cheered the nursing home so much that young children look forward to visiting grandpa or grandma, even when the old people are bedridden. It's no longer a scary, forbidding place for the young, who may be found there every day of the week.

To the surprise of some, the dog and cats and birds all get along. Sam and Shepherd, one of the cats, have become friends and chase each other up and down the hallways. Or perhaps a cockatiel will escape and fly through the hall. These events give the residents (and the staff) the variety of the unexpected.

Of course, not all residents are animal lovers; but for those with an aversion or allergies to animals, the staff is careful to keep the animals away. For those who like plants and animals, the effects have been startling. People who had been almost totally withdrawn and uncommunicative now smile and talk and laugh. One 102-year-old woman takes great delight in telling her daughters about her bird, Peter. In the beginning, she worried about having a bird because she couldn't take care of it. Now, she has something to talk about besides her aches and pains. And those have lessened—in spite of her great age.

Another woman, descending into dementia, had reverted to a time in her life when she had suffered abuse. She became frightened and would not look at people or speak above a whisper of more than one or two words. Then Riverview bought the cockatiels and named them George and Gracie. The withdrawn woman stood outside their cage teaching them their names. Then she began to speak with residents, and at last, has been seen conversing normally with total strangers.

The staff sees to the care of all the plants and animals. The Eden approach brings more work for the aides and the rest of the staff, but it began as, and remains, a volunteer effort. The Eden Alternative is at Riverview because everyone wants it and wants to help with it, even at the cost of added duties. Besides caring for the residents, each staff member has five bird cages to clean daily.

In addition to the indoor habitat, staff members plan to enhance the grounds of the one-story facility with native plants, in the hopes of encouraging wildlife to come and entertain the residents. Already they have put up enough bird feeders that every resident can enjoy the antics of wild birds, from bed, through the large windows. That 102-year-old woman especially enjoys watching them. Although nearly totally blind, she has enough peripheral vision to see the birds.

At both Riverview and outside, the wildlife sanctuary garden benefits everyone, human and nonhuman alike. It adds the necessary dimension to our existence: life. To live among living things and other live beings connects us to life on the grand scale. For wildlife gardeners, the pleasure it provides, coupled with the sense of making a contribution, of giving back to the planet instead of taking, may be one of the purest things we do. It's guilt-free and harmonious. It proves that doing the right thing can be loads of fun.

Chapter 8

Further Information

This book does not claim to have all the answers to all the questions about wildlife sanctuary gardening. It's merely the result of having lived with this kind of garden for more than a decade, learning the lessons it teaches, and looking for answers to my own questions. My search for information led me to some fascinating places, both among books in the public library and on the Internet.

With the information explosion upon us, we have no difficulty in finding information on whatever topic we wish to explore. Wildlife gardening is no exception. Not only are many fine books available on various aspects of this fascinating activity, the Internet brings you the entire world of wildlife gardening.

These days, anyone with access to a personal computer (PC) can search online library catalogs and the Internet. If you don't have a PC at home, your local public library probably has one you can use for research. Just ask the reference librarian for instructions on how to use it.

If you live in an urban area with more than one library branch, or if you live in a rural area where the nearest library may be fifty miles away, the book you want to read may not be conveniently located. You can search the library's online catalog and perhaps have the book sent directly to you or to the nearest branch of the public library.

Internet Searching

The Internet provides several different software programs by which you can search for information. These are known collectively as "search engines"; they travel the Internet pathways to find occurrences of the word or phrase you type. They don't search the documents themselves, ordinarily. Instead, they search parts of the files you don't see. These parts are called "meta tags," and they contain vital information about the file, such as the software used to make the HTML file, and the document's keywords.

When you search for a word or phrase (called a "search term"), the search engine tries to match it with the keywords in these meta tags. If your search term matches the keyword in a document, the search engine will count that document among its successes and return with a list of all available occurrences of the search term.

It's important to make your search term as specific as possible to the subject you want to research. If you type only *wildlife* or *garden,* the search engine will come back with thousands of documents, many of which may be irrelevant to what you're looking for. If you type *sanctuary gardening* the search engine may retrieve too few items.

I've used Metacrawler (www.metacrawler.com), Infoseek (www. infoseek.com), and Yahoo (www.yahoo.com). There are many other good search engines; I'm just not familiar with them. Each of the three I've used has a slightly different path that it follows in the Web to search the myriad connected servers where information is stored. (A Web server is a computer whose main function is to store information in a form that can be recognized and retrieved.) Each one of them has a slightly different form for the search terms.

With one search engine, for example, you enter a phrase in quotation marks, this way: "wildlife gardening." With another search engine you enter a phrase this way—wildlife AND gardening. The AND tells the search engine that you want a boolean search, i.e., that it should look for both words in the document.

When you search for information on wildlife sanctuary gardening, pay attention to the search engine's help system. Read about how it wants the search terms to be entered. You'll have more success that way, and fewer frustrations at not finding what you're looking for, or finding something you're not expecting.

What follows are lists of Web sites. The URLs (uniform resource locators—the "addresses" of the Web sites) are as accurate as I could make them, but servers change. Between the time this book went to press and the time you read it, the URL may have changed. Usually, the Webmaster (the person—male or female—who is responsible for maintaining the Web page) has updated the old address with the new one, but in case there's no message except "Not Found," enter the name of the Web site and let the search engine find it for you.

One last thing: This is by no means a complete list, but it'll get you started on your exciting quest for information on wildlife gardening and related subjects.

Organic Gardening Web Sites

The Natural Gardener
  www.bbg.org/gardening/natural/index.html

Organic Gardening Forum
  www.gardenweb.com/forums/organic

Urban Wildlife Web Sites

NSP – Bird Cam
  www.nspco.com/nspbird.htm
  (The Web site for viewing the peregrine falcons nesting on a highrise in Seattle)

National Wildlife Federation Home Page

www.nwf.org/	mailing address:
Wildlife Habitat Program:	89825 Leesburg Pike
www.nwf.org/habitats/	Vienna, VA 22184-001

National Institute for Urban Wildlife (references)
http://bordeaux.uwaterloo.ca/lcws/docs/referenc.html

Urban Wildlife Resources (MD)
www.erols.com/urbanwildlife/

Canadian Federation of Humane Societies
www.magi.com/~cfhs/about.htm

Texas Backyard Wildlife Program:
www.tpwd.state.tx.us/nature/plant/wldscape.htm
www.tpwd.state.tx.us/nature/plant/wldscapp.htm#wildsc
www.mcdef.org/bkecpm.htm

Chattanooga Nature Center
www.chattanooga.net/nature/index.html

Florida Wildlife Habitat Program
www.wec.ufl.edu/extension/HbtPrg.asp

Windstar Wildlife Institute
www.WindStar.org/wildlife

U.S. Department of Fish and Wildlife
www.fws.gov

Trumbull Land Trust (Frank Grazynski, Chm.)
www.geocities.com/RainForest/5496

Articles on the Internet

Hummingbirds
www.derived.com/~lanny/hummers

Web of Life
www.suite101.com/articles/article.cfm/3976

How to Make a Wildlife Garden
www.newciv.org/GIB/crespec/CS-113.HTML

Obtaining Native Plants
http://hammock.ifas.ufl.edu/txt/fairs/4724

Bird-Watching Sites

Baltimore Bird Club
  www.bcpl.lib.md.us

The Audubon Society
  www.audubon.org/

Seattle Audubon Society
  http://weber.u.washington.edu/~dvictor/aud.html

General Environmental Web Sites

Everything You Want to Know about Environmental Matters on the Web
  www.webdirectory.com/

Florida Internet Center for Understanding Sustainability
  www.ficus.usf.edu/default.htm

List of WWW Sites of Interest to Botanists
  http://biomserv.univ-lyon1.fr/botany/old/bot-uz.html#vz

List of WWW Sites of Interest to Ecologists
  http://biomserv.univ-lyon1.fr/ecology/ecology-pt.html

Web Sites Related to Wildlife Gardening

Grand Prairie Friends (An organization committed to preserving and
  restoring tallgrass prairie in east-central Illinois)
  www.prairienet.org/gpf/homepage.html

"How to Make a Forest Garden," by Patrick Whitefield (online article)
  www.newciv.org/GIB/crespec/CS-113.HTML

WSU Master Gardener: Stewardship Gardening
  http://gardening.wsu.edu/text/stew.htm

Wildlife Gardening - ICanGarden.com
  www.icangarden.com/Special_Interest/wl1.htm

Wild Ones Handbook: A Voice for the Natural Landscaping Movement
www.epa.gov/greenacres/wildones

Welcome to the McHenry County Defenders
www.mcdef.org/

The Gardens at Thunder Ridge
www.msn.fullfeed.com/~thunder/Garden/index.shtml

Plants of a Houston Urban Habitat
www.io.com/~pdhulce/Plantlist.HTML

Northern Prairie Biological Resources
www.npwrc.usgs.gov/resource/resource.htm

Massachusetts Horticultural Society
www.masshort.org/

Internet Forums Related to Wildlife Gardening

Ponds and Aquatic Plants Forum
www.gardenweb.com/forums/ponds

Garden Web Native Plant Forum
www.gardenweb.com/forums/natives

Nature Forum: The Wildlife Garden
www.nature.net/forums/garden

Native Plants in the Garden and Landscape
www.floridaplants.com/nati_garden.htm

Botanical Gardens and Arboreta

Your local arboretum can be an excellent source of information on which plants do well in a wildlife garden. For example, people in New York City might consult the Brooklyn Botanic Garden or the New York Botanical Garden in the Bronx. Another place to find information is from the Cornell University Cooperative Extension office in Manhattan. In San Francisco, Strybing Arboretum can provide excellent information. If you don't have such a resource at your doorstep (or a subway ride away), try the local branch of the library. If you don't know how to research this topic, ask at the reference desk for help on looking for plants that attract birds, bees, and butterflies. The reference librarian can be of great assistance.

American Association of Botanical Gardens and Arboreta
　　http://aabga.mobot.org/AABGA/

Arnold Arboretum at Harvard University (Massachusetts)
　　www.desert.net/museum/

Atlanta Botanical Garden (Georgia)
　　http://aabga.mobot.org/AABGA/Member.pages/Atlanta/atlanta.html

Bernheim Arboretum and Research Forest (Claremont, Kentucky)
　　www.win.net/bernheim/

MSU W. J. Beal Botanical Garden (East Lansing, Michigan)
　　www.cpp.msu.edu/beal.htm

Biltmore Estate (Asheville, North Carolina)
　　www.biltmore.com/G4.html
　　Note lists of plants and some wildlife, especially birds.

Botanica, the Wichita Botanical Gardens (Wichita, Kansas)
　　www.botanica.org/gardens.html
　　Note the woodland walk, butterfly garden, and wildflower garden.

Botanical Research Institute of Texas (Fort Worth, Texas)
　　www.Brit.ORG/lep
　　Note the landscape ecology program.

Brandywine River Museum (Chadds Ford, Pennsylvania)
　　http://aabga.mobot.org/AABGA/Member.pages/brandywine.html

Bowman's Hill Wildflower Preserve (New Hope, Pennsylvania)
　　http://aabga.mobot.org/AABGA/Member.pages/bowman.html

Boyce Thomson Southwestern Arboretum (Superior, Arizona)
　　http://ag.arizona.edu/BTA/

Luther Burbank Home and Gardens (Santa Rosa, California)
   http://aabga.mobot.org/AABGA/Member.pages/Burbank/lbhg.html
   Note a newly created wildlife garden.

Cedar Valley Arboretum and Botanical Gardens (Waterloo, Iowa)
   www.cedarnet.org/gardens/index.html#pgtop

Chicago Botanical Garden (Glencoe, Illinois)
   http://www.chicago-botanic.org/Explore.html
   See especially the naturalistic garden.

Chicago Wilderness (Chicago, Illinois)
   http://www.chiwild.org/

Cleveland Botanical Garden (Cleveland, Ohio)
   http://cbgarden.org
   See "Attracting Birds and Butterflies to Your Garden."

Connecticut College Arboretum Garden (New London, Connecticut)
   www.conncoll.edu/ccrec/greennet/arbo/welcome.html

Dallas Horticulture Center (Dallas, Texas)
   www.startext.net/homes/dhc

Denver Botanical Garden (Denver, Colorado)
   http://aabga.mobot.org/AABGA/Member.pages/Denver/denver.html

Desert Botanical Garden (Phoenix, Arizona)
   http://aabga.mobot.org/AABGA/Member.pages/desert.html

Descanso Gardens (La Cañada Flintridge, California)
   www.Descanso.com/Gateway.html

Devonian Botanical Garden (Edmonton, Alberta, Canada)
   www.discoveredmonton.com/devonian
   Emphasizes plants used by Northern Plains Indian tribes in the Native
   People's Garden

Dyck Arboretum of the Plains (Hesston, Kansas)
   www.hesston.edu/arbor
   Extensive collections of plants native to the Plains

Fairchild Tropical Gardens (Miami, Florida)
www.ftg.org

Florida Community College at Jacksonville Botanical Garden
(Jacksonville, Florida)
http://www1.fccj.cc.fl.us/Special/Garden/index.html
To support educational programs in horticulture and environmental
horticulture

University of Miami (Coral Gables, Florida)
http://fig.cox.miami.edu/Arboretum/gifford.html

Hawaii Tropical Botanical Garden (Hilo, Hawaii)
http://aabga.mobot.org/AABGA/Member.pages/hawaii.tropical.html

Heard Natural Science Museum and Wildlife Sanctuary (McKinney, Texas)
www.heardmuseum.org

Highstead Arboretum (Redding, Connecticut)
http://aabga.mobot.org/AABGA/Member.pages/highstead/
highstead.html

Holden Arboretum (Cleveland, Ohio)
www.holdenarb.org

The Huntington Library, Art Collections, and Botanical Gardens
(San Marino, California)
www.huntington.org

Huntsville–Madison County Botanical Garden (Huntsville, Alabama)
www.hsvbg.org/gardento.htm

Marie Selby Botanical Gardens (Sarasota, Florida)
www.hsvbg.org/gardento.htm

Frederik Meijer Gardens (Grand Rapids, Michigan)
http://aabga.mobot.org/AABGA/Member.pages/Meijer/meijer.html

Memorial University of Newfoundland (Newfoundland, Canada)
www.mun.ca/botgarden

Missouri Botanical Garden: Shaw Arboretum (St. Louis, Missouri)
www.mobot.org/MOBOT/arboretum/communities.html

Morton Arboretum (Lisle, Illinois)
www.mortonarb.org

Extension Services

To search the Internet, bring up your favorite search engine and search for "county extension service." This will produce a list of extension services around the country. Then, within these pages, search for the extension service for your state.

Cornell University
www.cce.cornell.edu/publications/catalog.html

Purdue Horticulture Extension Specialists
www.hort.purdue.edu/hort/ext/specialists.html

Wildlife Programs

Hudson Wildlife Programs
www.wildlifegarden.com/hudson.htm#programs

Akron (OH) Wildlife Programs:
- **Akron Zoo**
  (330) 375-2525
  500 Edgewood Ave.
  Akron, Ohio
- **Cuyahoga Valley National Recreation Area**
  (800) 445-9667
- **Wildlife Garden**
  (216) 342-3488
  130 W. Streetsboro St.
  Hudson, Ohio

Canton (OH) Area Wildlife Program Locations:

- **Canton Audubon Society**
  (330) 832-2491
  Meeting Location: Schoolhouse Junction 2705 Fulton Dr. N.W.
  Canton, Ohio
- **Jackson Community Parks**
  (330) 832-2845
  Jackson Township Hall
  5735 Wales Ave. N.W.
  Massillon, Ohio
- **Quail Hollow State Park**
  (330) 877-6652
  13340 Congress Lake Ave N. E.
  Hartville, Ohio
- **Sanders Nature Center**
  (330) 477-0448
  Sippo Lake Park
  800 Genoa Rd.
  Massillon, Ohio
- **The Wilderness Center**
  (330) 359-5235
  Wilmot, Ohio
- **Wildlife Garden—Canton**
  (330) 966-7666
  5860 Fulton Dr. N. W.
  Canton, Ohio

People and Plants and Spirituality

People-Plant Council
  www.hort.vt.edu/human/PPC.html

Community Lutheran Church Earthkeeping Ministry
  Mailing address: P.O. Box 1363
  Sterling, VA 20167

Earth Ministry (Connecting Christian faith and the environment)
    1305 NE 47th St.
    Seattle, WA 98105
    www.earthministry.org/

Eden Alternative
    www.edenalt.com

Urban Forestry

Urban Forestry: Reference Books
    www.ag.uiuc.edu/~forestry/guide/sec1.html

Urban Forestry: Newsletters
    www.ag.uiuc.edu/~forestry/guide/sec9.html

Urban Forestry: Bulletins, Pamphlets, and Fact Sheets
    www.ag.uiuc.edu/~forestry/guide/sec8.html

Native Plant Sites

U.S. Environmental Protection Agency
    www.epa.gov/grtlakes/greenacres

Purdue University
    Consumer Horticulture
    www.purdue.edu/ext/prairie_wildflowers.html

Ohio State University
    A Sense of Place
    www.hcs.ohio-state.edu/sense/Sense1.html

Native Plant Conservation Initiative
    www.aqd.nps.gov/natnet/npci

National Wildflower Research Center
    www.wildflower.org

Washington Native Plant Society
(with links to other native plant societies)
www.televar.com/~donew/natiplan/npslinks.html

Sites Listing Native Plant Societies:
www.televar.com/~donew/natiplan/plant_societies.html
Lists native plant societies of the United States
www.wildflower.org/native3.html
Lists native plant society Web sites
www.wildflower.org/native2.html
Lists gardens with displays of native plants
www.flmnh.ufl.edu/fnps/fnps6.htm
www.prairienet.org/gpf/natives.html

Native Plant Links (How to find more native plant resources)
www.wildflower.org/native3.html

Garden Web Native Plant Forum
www.gardenweb.com/forums/natives

The Garden Gate
www.prairienet.org/garden-gate

Native Plant Societies and Organizations

Arizona Native Plant Society
www.azstarnet.com/~anps

Connecticut Botanical Society
www.vfr.com/cbs

Florida Native Plant Society
www.flmnh.ufl.edu/fnps/fnps.htm

Georgia Botanical Society
www.mindspring.com/~jhitt/gbs.html

Idaho Native Plant Society
www.state.id.us/fishgame/inps1.htm

Grand Prairie Friends
   www.prairienet.org/gpf

Iowa Prairie Network
   www.netins.net/showcase/bluestem/ipnapp.htm

Kentucky Native Plant Society
   www.televar.com/~donew/natiplan/plant_societies.html

New England Wildflower Society
   www.ultranet.com/~newfs/newfs.html

Missouri Prairie Foundation
   www.moprairie.org

Native Plant Society of New Mexico, Otero Chapter
   www.wazoo.com/~dkeeney/npsoc.html

Central Ohio Native Plant Society
   www-obs.biosci.ohio-state.edu/cohplant.htm

Native Plant Society of Texas (NPSOT)
   http://bellnet.tamu.edu/Native3.htm

Native Plant Society of Texas, Austin
   http://lonestar.texas.net/~jleblanc/npsot_austin.html

Native Plant Society of Texas, Georgetown
   http://riceinfo.rice.edu/armadillo/Endanger/AOS/npst.html

Washington Native Plant Society
   www.wnps.org

Botanical Society of Washington (D.C.)
   www.fred.net/kathy/bsw.html

The Prairie Enthusiasts (Wisconsin)
   www.prairie.pressenter.com/

Native Plant Societies of the United States
   www.televar.com/~donew/natiplan/plant_societies.html

Native Plant Conservation Initiative (U.S. Government)
  www.televar.com/~donew/natiplan/plant_societies.html
  Peggy Olwell, Native Plant Conservation Initiative Chairperson
  1849 C Street, NW, Room 3223
  Washington, D.C. 20240-0001
  (202) 219-8933
  Or send an e-mail to native_plant@nps.gov. You will receive a packet containing a cooperator's agreement, general information about the initiative, and a meeting schedule.

Some native plant societies' mailing addresses may have changed by the time you read this. An up-to-date list can be found at the Web site of Native Plant Societies of the United States shown above.

Alabama Wildflower Society
  Route 2, Box 115
  Northport, AL 35476

Alaska Native Plant Society
  P.O. Box 14163
  Anchorage, AK 99514

Arizona Native Plant Society
  P.O. Box 41206, Sun Station
  Tucson, AZ 85717

Arkansas Native Plant Society
  Route 1, Box 282
  Mena, AR 71953

California Native Plant Society
  1722 J Street, Suite 17
  Sacramento, CA 95814

Colorado Native Plant Society
  Box 200
  Fort Collins, CO 80522

Connecticut Botanical Society
    10 Hillside Circle
    Storrs, CT 06268

Florida Native Plant Society
    P.O. Box 6116
    Spring Hill, FL 34606
    (813) 856-8202

North American Native Orchid Alliance
    P.O. Box 772121
    Ocala, Florida 34477-2121
    E-mail: NAORCHID@aol.com

Georgia Botanical Society
    1963 Ferry Drive NE
    Marietta, GA 30066-6250
    Phone: (770) 429-1836
    Fax: (770) 590-1108
    E-mail: ranger@america.net

Idaho Native Plant Society
    USDA-Forest, IF & RES
    316 East Myrtle Street
    Boise, ID 83706
    www2.state.id.us/fishgame/inps1.htm

Illinois Native Plant Society
    Forest Glen Preserve
    20301 E 900 North Road
    Westville, IL 61883

Indiana Native Plant and Wildflower Society
    c/o R. A. Ingraham
    6106 Kingsley Dr.
    Indianapolis, IN 46220

Kansas Wildflower Society
 Mulvane Art Center
 Washburn University
 17th & Jewell St.
 Topeka, KA 66621

Kentucky Native Plant Society
 Kentucky State Nature Preserve Commission
 801 Shenkel Lane
 Frankfort, KY 40601

Louisiana Native Plant Society
 Route 1, Box 151
 Saline, LA 71070

Josselyn Botanical Society
 Deering Hall, University of Maine
 Orono, ME 04469

Maryland Native Plant Society
 14720 Claude Lane
 Silver Spring, MD 20904

North American Sea Plant Society
 P.O. Box 262
 Feeding Hills, MA 01030-0262
 Fax: (413) 789-2076
 E-mail: nasps@aol.com

New England Wildflower Society
 Garden in the Woods
 180 Hemenway Rd.
 Framingham, MA 01701

New England Botanical Club
22 Divinity Avenue
Cambridge, MA 02138-2020

Michigan Botanical Club
c/o Herbarium, North University Building
University of Michigan
Ann Arbor, MI 48109-1057

Wildflower Association of Michigan
6011 W St Joseph, Suite 403
P.O. Box 80527
Lansing MI 48908-0527

Minnesota Native Plant Society
220 BioSci Center
University of Minnesota
1445 Gorter Avenue
St Paul, MN 55108
www.stolaf.edu/depts/biology/mnps

Mississippi Native Plant Society
c/o Ron Wieland
Miss. Museum of Natural Science
111 North Jefferson St.
Jackson, MS 39202

Missouri Native Plant Society
P.O. Box 20073
St Louis, MO 63144-0073

Montana Native Plant Society
P.O. Box 8783
Missoula, MT 59807-8782

Native Plant Society of Oregon
P.O. Box 902
Eugene, OR 97440

Northern Nevada Native Plant Society
    P.O. Box 8965
    Reno, NV 89507

Mojave Native Plant Society
    8180 Placid Dr.
    Las Vegas, NV 89123

New Jersey Native Plant Society
    c/o Frelinghuysen Arboretum
    P.O. Box 1295R
    Morristown, NJ 07960

Native Plant Society of New Mexico
    P.O. Box 5917
    Santa Fe, NM 87502

Niagara Frontier Botanical Society
    Buffalo Museum of Science
    1020 Humbolt Parkway
    Buffalo, NY 14211

New York Flora Association
    New York State Museum
    3132 CEC
    Albany, NY 12230

North Carolina Wildflower Preservation Society
    c/o NC Botanical Garden, UNC-CH
    Totten Center, 457-A
    Chapel Hill, NC 27514

Ohio Native Plant Society
    6 Louise Dr.
    Chagrin Falls, OH 44022

Oklahoma Native Plant Society
    2435 S. Peoria
    Tulsa, OK 74114

Pennsylvania Native Plant Society
P.O. Box 281
State College, PA 16804-0281

Southern Appalachian Botanical Society
c/o Charles Horn, Newberry College
2100 College St.
Newberry, SC 29108

South Carolina Native Plant Society (President: Rick Huffman)
P.O. Box 759
Pickens, SC 29671
(864) 868-7798

Tennessee Native Plant Society
c/o Department of Botany
University of Tennessee
Knoxville, TN 37916

Native Plant Society Of Texas
P.O. Box 891
Georgetown, TX 78627

El Paso Native Plant Society
7760 Maya Ave.
El Paso, TX 79912

Utah Native Plant Society
P.O. Box 520041
Salt Lake City, UT 84152

Virginia Native Plant Society
P.O. Box 844
Annadale, VA 22003

Washington Native Plant Society
P.O. Box 28690
Seattle, WA 98118-8690

West Virginia Native Plant Society
P.O. Box 2755
Elkins, WV 26241

Wyoming Native Plant Society
1604 Grand Ave.
Larimie, WY 82070

Botanical Society of Washington
Department of Biology-NHB/166
Smithsonian Institution
Washington, DC 20560

(U.S. Government) Native Plant Conservation Initiative
1849 C St. NW, Rm 3223
Washington, DC 20240
E-mail: native_plant@nps.gov

Control of Exotic Plants and Animals

Society for Ecological Restoration
http://nabalu.flas.ufl.edu/ser/SERhome.html

U.S. Department of the Interior
www.doi.gov/news/weed.html

U.S. Bureau of Land Management
www.blm.gov/education/weed/whats_a_weed.html

Books

North Woods: An Inside Look at the Nature of Forests in the Northeast by Peter J. Marchand (Boston: AMC Books, 1987).

Growing California Native Plants by Marjorie G. Schmidt (California Natural History Guides Series No. 45, Berkeley: University of California Press, 1980).

Southern Gardens, Southern Gardening by William Lanier Hurt (Durham, NC: Duke University Press, 1992).

Gardening in the South with Don Hastings:

Vol. I: Trees, Shrubs and Lawns (Dallas, TX: Taylor Publishing Company, 1987).

Vol. III: Flowers, Vines and Houseplants (Dallas, TX: Taylor Publishing Company, 1991).

Index

More great books for gardeners from Ten Speed Press

Brother Crow, Sister Corn
Traditional American Indian Gardening
Carol Buchanan
An in-depth look at how Native Americans traditionally gardened, along with dozens of Native songs and myths about the earth.
6 x 9 inches • 136 pages with color insert • $11.95 paper • ISBN 0-89815-850-8

How to Grow More Vegetables*
*Than You Ever Thought Possible on Less Land Than You Can Imagine
John Jeavons
This pioneering work is internationally renowned as the best work on biointensive gardening for individuals. Now in a revised fifth edition, with over 300,000 copies in print in seven languages.
8½ x 11 inches • 192 pages • $16.95 paper • ISBN 0-89815-767-6

The Sustainable Vegetable Garden
A Backyard Guide to Healthy Soil and Higher Yields
John Jeavons and Carol Cox
This "quick and dirty" introduction to biointensive gardening shows how easy it is to grow organic fruits and vegetables in any little plot of land. A revolutionary approach to feeding ourselves and nurturing the planet.
7⅜ x 9¼ inches • 128 pages • $11.95 paper • ISBN 1-58008-016-2

Dead Snails Leave No Trails
Natural Pest Control for Home and Garden
Loren Nancarrow and Janet Taylor
Simple and effective natural pest-control methods for chemical-free gardening, including beneficial plants, eliminating ants, roaches, and rodents indoors and out, nontoxic flea relief for pets, and more.
6 x 9 inches • 160 pages • $11.95 paper • ISBN 0-89815-852-4

The Worm Book

The Complete Guide to Gardening and Composting with Worms
Loren Nancarrow and Janet Taylor
Everything you need to do to build your own worm bin, make your garden worm-friendly, pamper your soil, and much more.
6 x 9 inches • 160 pages • $11.95 paper • ISBN 0-89815-994-6

Introduction to Permaculture
Bill Mollison with Reny Mia Slay
This book weaves together hands-on techniques of soil, agricultural, and livestock management, earth-friendly irrigation, and more, to form a clear and inspiring picture of how sustainable agriculture can work.
7¾ x 10¾ inches • 224 pages • $16.95 paper • ISBN 0-908228-08-2

Available from your local bookstore, or by ordering direct from the publisher. Call or write for our catalogs of over 1,000 books, posters, and tapes.

Ten Speed Press • Celestial Arts • Tricycle Press
Box 7123, Berkeley, California 94707
Order phone (800) 841-2665 • Fax (510) 559-1629
order@tenspeed.com • www.tenspeed.com